Slices of South Wales

is a wonderful way to reunite yourself with many of the events that through time have thrust the region into the spotlight. People and places feature significantly too, in a fascinating compendium of words and pictures recording everyday life and events that have had an impact down many years.

Slices of South Wales is no ordinary look back in time. Instead it unveils a fresh and vibrant approach to happenings that played a big part in the lives of all those who experienced them. For those who didn't, the accounts of a rare mix of writers — some well known, others not so — offers a unique glimpse of how life was.

Alongside this, a selection of fascinating facts and items that were once a part of nearly everyone's daily lives, lies waiting to be discovered. Anyone who has ever lived in or loved South Wales will discover that as they turn the pages of this book, they will be whisked away on their very own special, magical mystery tour.

Although of serious intent Slices of South Wales presents its content in a manner akin to the children's annuals of days gone by, but assembled with adults in mind; it is a magazine, but within the covers of a book; best of all it is the kind of publication that can be picked up and put down again at leisure. Most importantly it is a compilation that will be enjoyed by young and old alike.

Compiled by David Roberts

First published in Great Britain in 2013
by Bryngold Books Ltd.,
100 Brynau Wood, Cimla,
Neath, South Wales SA11 3YQ.

www.bryngoldbooks.com

Typesetting, layout,
editing and design
by Bryngold Books

ISBN 978-1-905900-30-5

Printed in
South
Wales
by Stephens and George
Print Group

Slices of South Wales

Sun, sea and... sand

COLIN SCOTT recalls distant days when families clambered aboard almost endless convoys of buses to join the exodus from the valleys to favourite seaside destinations.

In the 1950s and 1960s, before most South Wales families had a car, Sunday bus trips to the seaside from scores of valley communities were extremely popular. Sunday schools, workingmen's clubs, institutes and societies of all kinds organised outings for their members. These day trips to Paradise saw a virtual exodus to the coastal resorts of Barry Island, Porthcawl and Aberavon Beach.

Thousands of people would be on the move for a day at the beach and the funfair, and no doubt a few pubs and cafes too, for good measure. Buses and coaches in a plethora of colours allied to the various valleys municipalities and both private and public transport undertakings ran in long, impressive and seemingly endless convoys to the coast every summer weekend.

Dozens of buses and coaches ran down to Barry from the Monmouthshire valleys, while the mid-Glamorganshire communities piled aboard a fleet of the Rhondda Transport Company's double deckers for the shorter journey to Porthcawl or Aberavon Beach. Buses stretched from one end of the street to the other and quickly filled up as excited children, with half-a-crown of spending money and a bottle of Tizer, piled aboard. Each vehicle carried a label with the bus number, often reaching the 30s and 40s. If your memory was good you remembered the number and avoided the risk of ending up at perhaps Croesyceiliog instead of Blackwood or Bargoed.

Aberavon Beach, in its 1960s heyday.

Once under way, the buses weaved their way down the valleys, sometimes on roads that were not used by regular services. Collisions with over-hanging tree branches could be a nasty experience, and on more than one occasion a journey was tragically curtailed by an unexpected low bridge. Youths would gather at the back of the upper deck, where the emergency rear

Barry Island

Porthcawl

window was dropped open for air – and for whistling at the girls as they passed!

Eventually the first cry went out from the top deck: 'I can see the sea!' But then, just as the journey seemed over, the queues began, with so many buses trying to park up for the day – at Barry Island behind the railway station; in Porthcawl, the Salt Lake park near the miniature railway, while in Aberavon the buses rested in sand-filled parks along the length of the seafront, where the Afan Belle open-top double decker would convey you along to Miami Beach funfair.

At the end of the day the game of Hunt the Bus would be played out. The trek home saw the last of the sand-blasted sandwiches distributed, as lobster-coloured legs stuck to the seats and faces matched the colour of the bus. Usually the return home coincided nicely with the opening of the 'workies' club, where weary dads took shelter until Mam had bathed the kids and put them to bed, and all returned to normal at the end of a memorable fun-filled day out.

Switched on Tredegar firm led the way

While the rest of the world marvelled at the idea of electric vehicles, the people of Tredegar helped turn the dream into reality recalls KEITH ROBERTS.

WHEN the first model left a brand new Tredegar vehicle manufacturing factory on a spring day in 1968 it carried with it bright hopes of a long and successful future.

The company behind the project, Morrison-Electricar, hoped it would herald the start of a major production facility in the town leading to thousands of similar battery-powered electric vehicles being made at the plant every year.

Unfortunately for the firm, the people it employed and the town of Tredegar itself, the far-reaching concept of mass-produced electric commercial vehicles was simply not appropriate for the 1970s. It was to be another 30 years before the idea began to take off as concerns mounted about global warming and pollution.

By then it was too late for Morrison-Electricar. Its products were revolutionary, but in the 1970s and early 1980s they were too far ahead of their time and the dream ended with the closure of the Tredegar factory in early 1983. The reason was simply changing lifestyles. The day of the supermarket had dawned and families preferred to take their cars to the shops rather than have doorstep milk and bread deliveries. Many tradespeople used electric vehicles and fewer customers for them meant they needed fewer vehicles. Coupled with the fact that milk floats and similarly powered electric vehicles were

The factory at Tredegar from which the valleys led the world.

Morrison Electricar vehicles that were popular in the valleys.

extremely robust – they could last 30 years and more – demand for new models dropped dramatically.

All this could not have been forseen in the 1960s. Battery-powered electric vehicles were not new and there was a proven demand for them. In August 1967, a year before the Tredegar plant opened, the Electric Vehicle Association of Great Britain claimed that Britain had more of these vehicles on its roads than the rest of the world put together.

Morrison-Electricar, which had its origins in Leicester, thrived through the end of Victorian times, two World Wars, the Depression, and the mass of changes in the 1950s and 1960s. In 1941 the company standardised on three types of body which become the basis for

The comforting sounds delivered with the early morning pinta!

MILK floats were by far the most numerous battery-powered electric vehicles in South Wales in the years from the Second World War to the mid-1980s.

They were popular both with dairy firms which had large fleets of vehicles and the sole, independent milkman with a small round and just one float. No-one really knows why they are called milk floats, but one suspects it is because they are so quiet and move so slowly-a float's top speed is between 15 and 20 mph-that they appear to be floating along the road.

All milk floats, whichever firm made them, looked broadly similar and were instantly recognisable. But you were far more likely to hear them than see them.

A milkman's round started early in the morning, usually well before daylight. If you happened to be awake before it was time to get up, you might hear the reassuring sound of the deliveries being made. The float would arrive making a 'click, whir, whine, whir, click', sound. This would be followed by muffled footsteps and a chink of glass as the milkman picked up the empties left out overnight for collection on the doorstep and replaced them with full bottles.

Then there would be more muffled footsteps followed by a louder 'ker-chunk' as the milkman put the empties into one of the crates at the back of his float. The whine of the float would start up again and the whole process was re-enacted a few yards away.This would continue with the sounds becoming fainter and fainter as the milkman moved up the street until they disappeared altogether. By then you knew it was time to get up.

Sadly, this scene has become increasingly rare. Some 30 years ago 85 per cent of milk was sold on the doorstep. Now it is just eight per cent. Today we are all more likely to go to the supermarket for our bread, milk and dairy products.

There are still dozens and dozens of small, delivery businesses across South Wales and these days you can use them to order more than just bread and dairy items. Now they can supply more than 150 products all to the front door.

thousands of battery-powered electric milk floats built after the war. There were other UK electric vehicle manufacturers but Morrison-Electricar was the largest and one of the most successful. It was full order books that first brought it to Tredegar in the 1960s. It had outgrown its production facility in Leicester and there were problems finding a bigger plant in the area. Harold Wilson's Labour government of 1966-70 had set up development areas in those parts of the country hard hit by the rundown in traditional industries and the South Wales valleys, which lost thousands of coal mining jobs in the 1960s, was one of them.
Major efforts were underway to encourage new employers to set up around valley towns and when the Board of Trade offered to build Morrison-Electricar a purpose-built plant in Tredegar, the company leapt at the chance.

So on February 1, 1967, work began on an 82,000 sq ft state-of-the-art factory on the Dukestown Industrial Estate. It was capable of producing 2,500 vehicles every year which, at a rate of eight or nine a day, seems particularly optimistic in the light of later events. A specially constructed vehicle test track was built around the plant and the products were put though their paces.

Doorstep delivery by Morrison-Electricar milk float.

What especially endeared the firm to Wilson's government was that the new plant included a design and development department in the basement. The 'white heat' of new technology was particularly important to the Prime Minister and so it was with extraordinary high hopes that the Secretary of State for Wales, George Thomas, performed the plant's official opening ceremony on October 11, 1968.

The full range of Morrison-Electricar products was put on display for the day. There was the traditional milk float, a special bakery and confectionary delivery van, a parcel van, a mobile butcher's, a mobile medical research laboratory, a refuse collection lorry and a 25-seat electric bus.

Business looked good for the first few years and new products were introduced, including a pick-up van designed at the Tredegar plant. A dapper Lord Snowden visited the factory in July 1974 and drove a milk float around the test track.

But in the second half of the 1970s demand from dairies, bakers, laundry services and councils for new electric vehicles slowed drastically and Morrison-

Powering the Pope

MOST electric vehicles in South Wales were used to deliver milk or bread, with those owned by the Co-op and Mothers Pride being among the most common.

The Co-operative Society had been using electric vehicles since the 1930s and built up a close partnership with Morrison-Electricar.

The company's milk floats and electric bread vans were particularly popular with the Cardiff CRS and South Wales CRS and the later blue-and-white vehicles with prominent Co-op logos on the sides were familiar sights all across the area.

Mother's Pride delivered bread throughout South Wales and its red-and-white electric vans could be seen in daily service. But when Morrison-Electricar opened its Tredegar plant in 1968 it had a much more extensive and ambitious portfolio. There were two electric buses which went on trial in several UK towns and cities, although their limited range before their batteries needed charging meant they were ultimately unsuccessful.

Morrison-Electricar also had a range of industrial trucks and could supply mobile butchery and refuse collection vehicles.

The company had a high profile across the UK and this was given a major boost when Pope John Paul visited Pontcanna Fields in Cardiff on June 2,1982, the first ever visit to the UK by a reigning pontiff.

Two of its new dairy delivery vans were painted in the papal colours of yellow and white and used in the communion service attended by thousands of worshippers.

A line up of some of the Morrison-Electricar vehicles used by Cardiff Co-operative Society.

Electricars, by now renamed Crompton Electricars, began to target the market for mass produced vans whose deliveries were within 50 miles.The last product was the NP10, designed at Tredegar in 1981-2, which it was hoped would result in new demand from commercial enterprises for local work.

It looked a good product and trials were going well but suddenly at the end of 1982, Hawker-Siddeley, which now owned the company, put the business up for sale for £3 million. A firm in the Midlands took over, but not the Tredegar plant which was owned by the Welsh Development Agency, the government's job creation enterprise that had succeeded the Board of Trade in Wales.

The factory closed in early 1983 with around 160 job losses and the machinery was shipped out to the Midlands. The dream had ended after fewer than 15 years and yet it is possible to wonder what would have happened in Tredegar if the events of 1967 had taken place in 2007. Recent years have seen a surge of interest in battery-powered electric vehicles amid concerns about emissions from petrol and diesel vehicles and global warming. Electric bus trials are under way in a number of UK towns and cities and it is estimated each will cut tail pipe emissions by around 500 tonnes a year. Electric vehicles cost more to buy but a diesel bus costs £23,000 a year to run while its electric equivalent costs just £10,000 and also has lower maintenance costs.

Mainstream car manufacturers, including Ford and Nissan, have produced electric vehicles and a 50-strong fleet of all-electric taxi cabs has been ordered for London.

The growth in internet shopping continues and electric vehicles are ideally suited as the low cost and less polluting way to make home deliveries. Electric milk floats are low carbon and are exempt from road tax. They cost just 10p a mile to run.

All these exciting developments might have come Tredegar's way, but its day dawned 30 years too soon. We can only speculate on what might have been.

There wasn't much that couldn't be delivered by one of the company's vehicles!

A 1960s bride steps out for the photographer, her dress and shoes admirably mirroring the time.

Flowers played a big part in this 1920s Swansea wedding it seems.

Aisles of STYLE

For many young South Wales women a white wedding is the stuff of their dreams. Surprisingly, though, white hasn't always been the height of fashion.

A quick look back through the pages of fashion history books shows that most colours of the rainbow have played their part through the fullness of time.

In the 17th and 18th Centuries, yellow was very popular, though at the same time lower class brides often wore grey as they were able to wear it again and again as Sunday best.

The traditional wedding dress as we know it first appeared in the late 18th century when machine fabrics and cheap muslin were imported from India. The Roaring Twenties saw convention cast to the wind and at the same time hemlines said goodbye to the ankle and hello to the knee. Wedding dress styles also changed and gowns became shorter than ever before although some believed that these were unworthy of a church marriage so the traditional floor length dresses also stayed in fashion among many.

. . . but the beautiful bride didn't always wear a traditional white gown!

Mr Tom Phillips and his bride Fanny Pickering with attendants at their 1924, Neath wedding.

The white wedding dress all but disappeared during the austere times brought on by the outbreak of the Second World War. Clothing rations were introduced in 1941 and some brides borrowed gowns from relatives while others wore uniform.

The 1950s brought ballerina length dresses held out with stiff petticoats, there were many variations of this. Some women dyed their petticoat after the wedding for use as a cocktail dress. However Many brides still wore the traditional wedding dress.

The Swinging Sixties brought a plethora of vivid styles and colour seemed to be the champion throughout, while in the 1970s sleeves were a big feature, Princess Ann led the way with her Tudor style sleeves and brides followed by having sleeves from every era.

The wedding of Princess Diana to Prince Charles in the 1980s ushered in yet another nod to Victorian fashion. Diana's billowing skirts with cathedral-length train and large veil brought romanticism back to wedding fashion. Brides enamoured

Neath couple Frank Pickering and Vi Lane at their wedding in 1921.

A typical South Wales wedding group from the 1920s.

The wedding of Prince Charles and Lady Diana sparked many new trends for 1980s weddings.

Mary Morgan was the bride at this Neath wedding in 1945.

with the look dismissed frugality in favour of the fairy-tale gown. With this shift in priorities, wedding gowns became intricately detailed and far more expensive. Modern day wedding gowns are as diverse as the brides who wear them.

Embroidery and beading with a stiffly corseted satin bodice became a huge hit in the 1990s with the all important sleeves adapted to be off the shoulder for many brides.

In the 21st century the majority of brides choose strapless gowns, often ivory in colour. The modern wedding gown has been more than 200 years in the making and preserved vintage samples offer a rich strand of our fashion history. For many they will evoke strong feelings of nostalgia for that all-important, but now distant, special day.

– **CHERYL ROBERTS**

Clock watching

Time – and tide – or so they say, wait for no man. And that's why the countless civic and public clocks to be found right across South Wales have played such an important part in so many lives – for such a long time too. Even to this day many people rely on the accuracy of these often magnificent time-pieces to keep them on track in their busy daily lives. Such clocks can be found on civic buildings, churches, public monuments, even hotels. They can be seen at railway stations, over theatres and often can be viewed from a great distance. Whatever their individual appearance or role they all share the one defined purpose of helping ensure we arrive at our destination on time. For many people they become old friends in community life. When they vanish they are sadly missed. They are all part of the rich cultural history and heritage of South Wales.

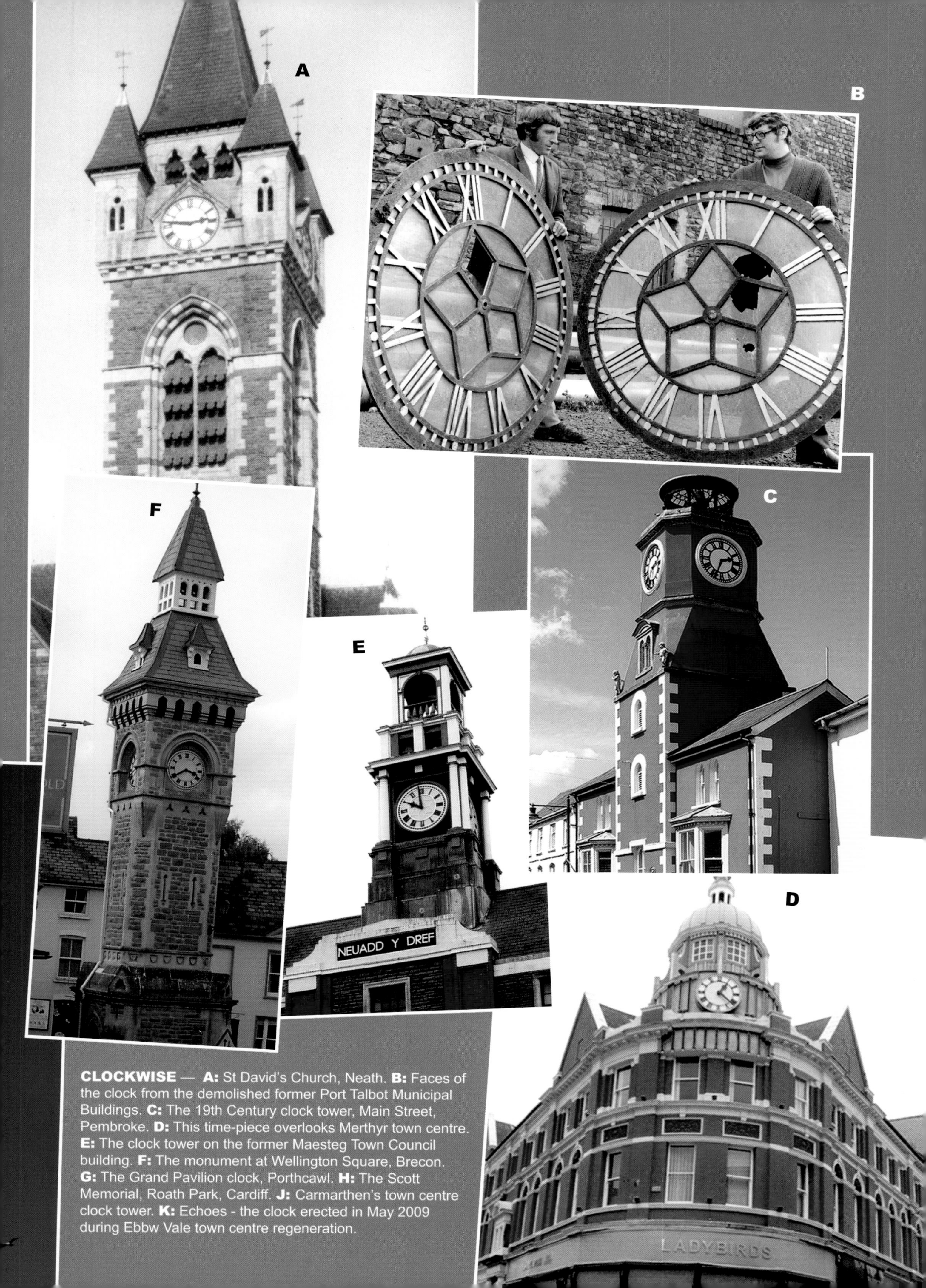

CLOCKWISE — A: St David's Church, Neath. **B:** Faces of the clock from the demolished former Port Talbot Municipal Buildings. **C:** The 19th Century clock tower, Main Street, Pembroke. **D:** This time-piece overlooks Merthyr town centre. **E:** The clock tower on the former Maesteg Town Council building. **F:** The monument at Wellington Square, Brecon. **G:** The Grand Pavilion clock, Porthcawl. **H:** The Scott Memorial, Roath Park, Cardiff. **J:** Carmarthen's town centre clock tower. **K:** Echoes - the clock erected in May 2009 during Ebbw Vale town centre regeneration.

Pier-ing

WE do like to be beside the seaside, we do like to be beside the sea . . . and for many in South Wales that often meant a trip to the nearest pleasure pier. JONATHAN ISAACS looks at the two survivors of this wonderful Victorian attraction on the southern coast of Wales — Mumbles, seen here, and Penarth.

LET'S imagine the year is 1895, it is summer and we are taking a ferry trip from Cardiff around the bay to the peaceful and popular Victorian resort of Penarth.

Our transport is the regular ferry service between Cardiff and Penarth which has been operated since 1856 by the Cardiff Steam and Navigation Company. In previous years we would have had to get off at Penarth using a landing stage on wheels which was hauled up the beach, but in February 2013, work was completed on a cast iron and timber deck pleasure pier which has a landing jetty from where we can disembark for our day out away from the noise and pollution of industrial Cardiff and the valleys.

The new 658-ft long Penarth Pier is the centrepiece of our visit and we can stroll along its promenade admiring splendid views across the channel, to the islands of Flatholm and Steepholm and further on to Weston-super-Mare which has its own pleasure pier.

into the past

Mumbles

Later we might take a pleasant walk along Penarth's esplanade and cliffs, mingling with thousands of others who are savouring the delights of this peaceful resort, promoted in Victorian times as 'The Garden by the Sea'. They will have come from all over South Wales, the Midlands and the West Country, probably by train, and the new pier's landing jetty will be a major boost for the lucrative steam ship trade across the Bristol Channel.

Before we return to the pier for our ferry home we might rest awhile in the seafront gardens or sit on the sandy beach watching the muddy coloured waters lap gently to the shore.

Our imaginary day out is typical of the way people in South Wales would have spent some of their leisure time in Victorian and Edwardian times and piers were a major attraction. To encourage even more visitors, Penarth Pier was further developed in the early years of the twentieth century.

A wooden pavilion was built at the seaward end in 1907, shelters and shops were added and a concrete landing stage was completed in 1927-8. The piece de resistance was the art deco pavilion which was built as a majestic entrance to the pier in 1929.

This was Penarth Pier's heyday and as well as day visitors it hosted many concerts and dances.

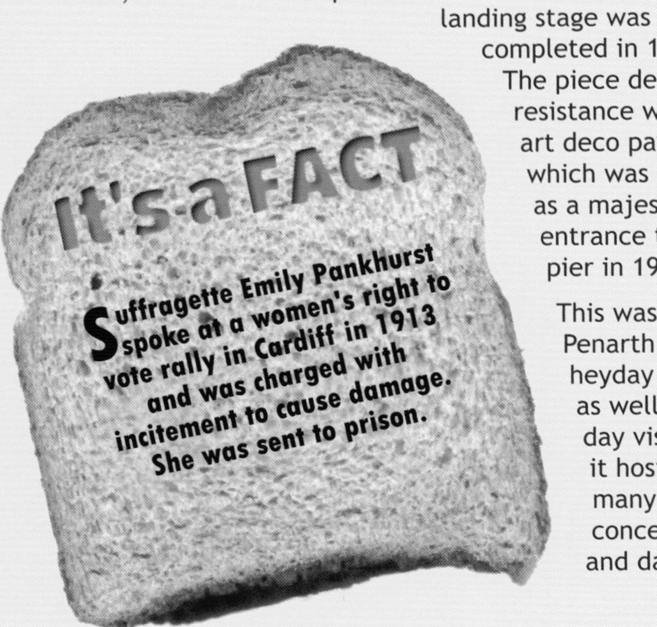

But it has not all been sun and joy. The pier's history is loaded with incident and what could have been a major tragedy was narrowly averted by the bravery of the rescue services on August Bank Holiday Monday in 1931. That night around 200 people were doing the foxtrot in the wooden pavilion at the seaward end when a major blaze broke out, probably caused by a carelessly discarded cigarette.

Hundreds more people were enjoying a variety show in the art deco pavilion and for a time it seemed likely that a disaster was imminent.

The wooden pavilion, shelters, shops and decking were destroyed by the flames, but amazingly all 800 people on the pier that night were saved thanks to a dramatic sea and land rescue. The fire didn't burn out for three days, but thankfully the art deco pavilion survived.

The pier was rebuilt at the then sizeable cost of £3,157 but that was not the last of the tragedies. A 7,130 tonne Canadian cargo steamship collided with the pier during severe gales in 1947 causing serious damage. It cost £28,000 to repair and the pier did not re-open until 1950.

Then in August 1966 the paddle steamer, Bristol Queen, collided with the pier in dense fog and caused £25,000 damage. Thankfully Penarth Pier has survived the mishaps. Substantial renovations, including work on the steelwork, decking and facilities, has ensured its long term future.

The wooden pavilion was never rebuilt after the fire but prospects are bright for the art deco pavilion which has been sadly neglected over recent years. A multi-million pound refurbishment scheme is under way on this iconic building which will see it reopen as a cinema, cafe, observatory and multi-purpose community complex.

Penarth Pier, built for the Victorian age, is being redeveloped for the 21st century.

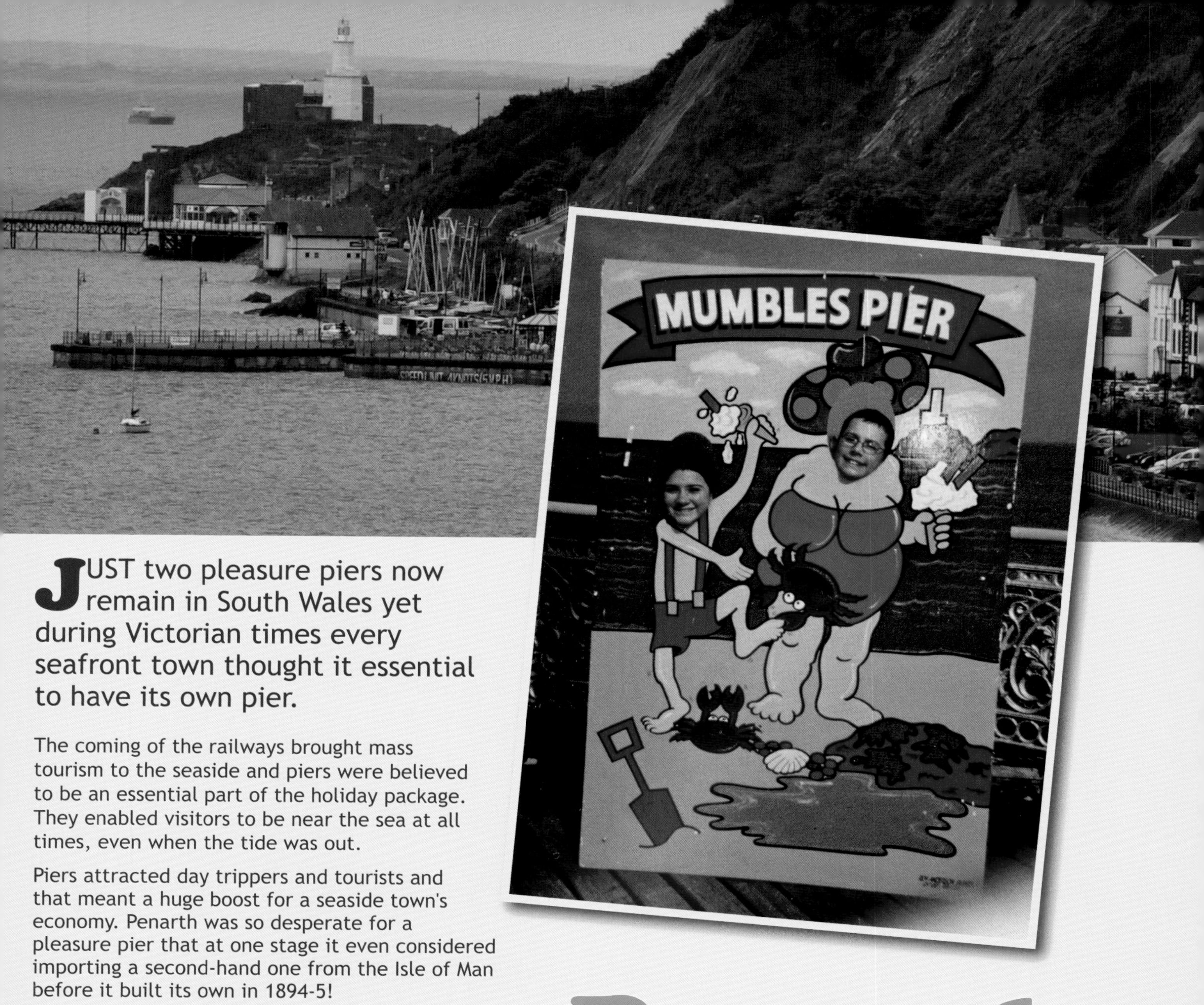

JUST two pleasure piers now remain in South Wales yet during Victorian times every seafront town thought it essential to have its own pier.

The coming of the railways brought mass tourism to the seaside and piers were believed to be an essential part of the holiday package. They enabled visitors to be near the sea at all times, even when the tide was out.

Piers attracted day trippers and tourists and that meant a huge boost for a seaside town's economy. Penarth was so desperate for a pleasure pier that at one stage it even considered importing a second-hand one from the Isle of Man before it built its own in 1894-5!

No fewer than 101 piers were built in Wales and England between 1814 and 1957, the first was at Ryde on the Isle of Wight, but today just 55 survive and the future of 10 of these is uncertain.

Bangor, Beaumaris on Anglesey, Colwyn Bay, Llandudno, Mumbles, Penarth and the Royal Pier in Aberystwyth make up the Welsh list of surviving piers.

The future for Colwyn Bay looks uncertain and it is too late for Aberavon Pier which opened in

Penarth

1898, was closed during the Second World War and demolished in 1962, and for Tenby Pier which opened in 1899, was also closed during the war, and demolished between 1946 and 1953.

But prospects look brighter for the others including Mumbles Pier which just a few years' ago was very much on the endangered list.

It was suffering from the malady that afflicts all Victorian pleasure piers, decay and the enormous cost of repairs. Yet in its heyday it was a mecca for visitors, not just from Swansea but from across South Wales. Opened on May 10, 1898, at a cost of £10,000, the 835ft long Mumbles Pier was also the terminus of the world's oldest passenger railway, the Swansea and Mumbles Railway, which brought thousands of visitors every week during the height of summer.

But this figure declined when the railway closed on January 5,1960, by which time the pier had undergone extensive reconstruction work with a new landing jetty added. The pier owners, Amusement Equipment Co Ltd, have spent many thousands of pounds on maintenance and repairs over the years and a new pavilion was built on the landward side of the pier in 1998. Even so, the repair bills were continuing to rise, some of the pier's

Crowds throng Penarth's promenade at the height of its popularity.

side rails and seating were rusting away and major restoration work was required. The pier's future looked in jeopardy until a multi-million pound development scheme was approved and its future prospects given a huge boost.

The National Piers Society was founded in 1979 under the leadership of the late poet laureate, Sir John Betjeman, a passionate advocate for Victorian architecture. The society campaigns to fight for the future of our pleasure piers.

It says: “The seaside piers around the coast of Britain stand as a powerful reminder of the achievements of Victorian engineers and entrepreneurs.”

Those in South Wales certainly bear that out.

Amen to all Andy!

— glad to leave the screaming behind him

Home-grown guitar man and former 1960s teen idol Andy Fairweather Low tells GRACE TAYLOR about his earliest musical awakenings in Cardiff.

ANDY Fairweather Low is at pains to point out that the kind of rabid, screaming teen stardom he found back in the early 1960s with Amen Corner is something he was happy to leave behind.

Invariably suited and booted he still cuts a sharp figure some 50 years later, and that voice and those guitar skills speak for themselves.

But there is still something of the bashful lad about him and I imagine being in the midst of a deafening throng while roaring through Gin House elicited some discomfort from him.

But despite being the go-to man when a rock legend is looking for a killer guitar player with a rangy, soulful, R&B wail and a hip musical education, one thing he hasn't left behind is his roots.

Born in Ystrad Mynach, raised in Cardiff, and living there still in Rhiwbina, the 64-year-old's onstage banter often recalls memories of sticky-floored, sticky-bodied gig nights at The Ritz in Skewen or of the Afan Lido. And the Welsh flag is always somewhere to be found on stage when he and his current crew, The Low Riders, do their thing.

Like many people of the same vintage, Andy's earliest musical awakenings came courtesy of that big childhood treat of the Saturday Morning Picture Show, in his neighbourhood cinema. Along with the manly heroics of Zorro and Tarzan came a good dose of pop, he remembers.

"It would be the teenage show at the Capitol for sixpence on a Saturday morning," he said.

"We would get magic, film and live music; a Shadows-type group, a Joe Brown-type player and a Helen Shapiro-type singer and it all took place in the cinema."

One of the hallmarks of Andy's solo, post Amen Corner career has been the quirky cover version. And those songs he heard as a kid stuck with him like a tattoo.

One blessed studio session saw him, for instance, record Travelling Light as if it were a classic, croony Don Gibson country song.

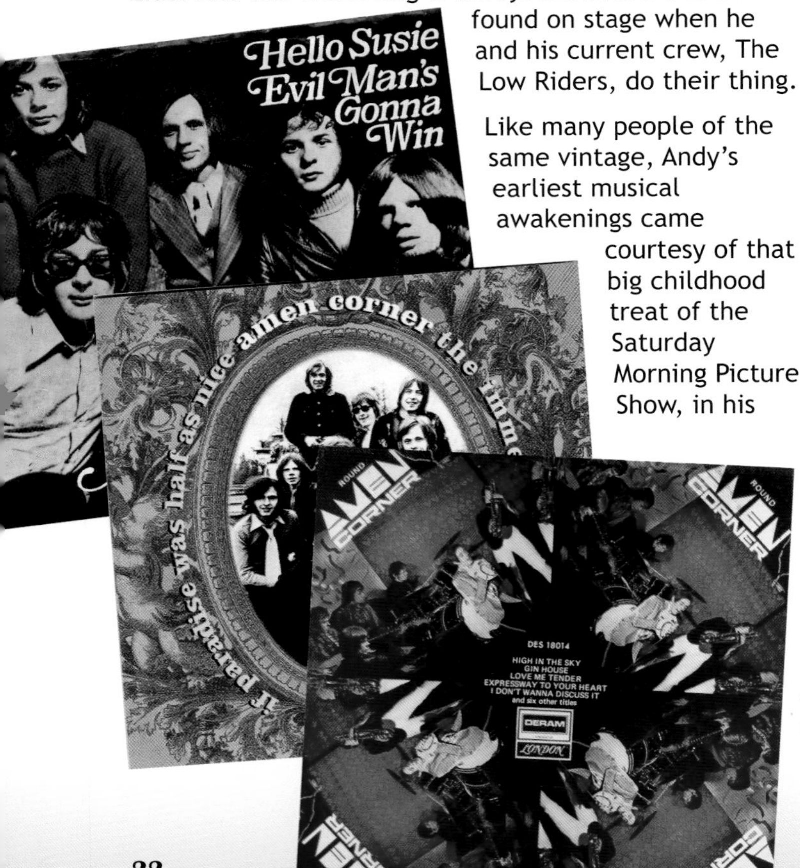

COVER VERSIONS: How the vinyl was packed at the height of Amen Corner's musical magnificence.

that, says

Skill and sound

He may be suited and booted now, but for Andy Fairweather Low the skill and the sound are still there. ***Pictures: Judy Totton.***

"I'm still in love with the songs I heard when I was growing up," he explains, "like Cliff's Travelling Light and even Bachelor Boy.

"When I hear that song I'm back on holiday in Margate.

"And Frank Ifield, when I hear him, I immediately get the smell of the Hoover going on and the roast in the oven. That's why music is so special."

But a teenage brush with some less clean-cut more hedonistic noise-makers put the seal on it for young Andy.

Somehow his school books, from Llanrumney Secondary Modern, didn't call to him quite as alluringly as the chugging, throaty guitar work of a simian-looking stage prowler called Keith. Making music was going to be Andy's life.

"Somebody took me to see the Rolling Stones at Sophia Gardens, and it was all over." he admits. The Stones shared a bill with Bern Elliot and with the moody twang-meister from The Shadows, Jet Harris.

Top of the South Wales pops

Mary Hopkin

Shakin' Stevens

Bonnie Tyler

Ricky Valance

If you were a teenager and into pop there was only one thing to do with your bedroom wall – plaster it with pictures of your idols scissored from your favourite mag, just like this.

After the show Andy borrowed a friend's guitar, got his fingers around some Chuck Berry riffs and picked up an early taste of life at the mic at the Kennard Rooms in Cardiff's Albany Road, heading up the valleys too.

"I've been blessed – especially when I think about the options open to me when I was at school," he says.

"I remember going into one GCE, writing my name on the top of the exam paper and not being able to answer any of the questions. I hadn't revised, but was up all night trying to play like Keith Richards.

"I remember my mum asking me how I did in my exams and I said: 'Yeah I think it went well', knowing I'd have a little grace before the results came in. By that time I was gone, playing in London.

"By then, I was playing two or three nights a week. I had very little talent but that didn't stop me."

His mid-1960s apprenticeship was worked out at The Ritz in a band called the Sect Maniacs, with Dave Edmunds' Poundsticks and Swansea's The Corncrackers, working the same scene.

At that time too, young Andy was working at Barratt's music shop in Cardiff's Wyndham Arcade, admiring its shiny stock, and paying for his first guitar on HP.

Night times saw him limber up in his first bands – the Firebrands, the TaffBeats and the Sect Maniacs, all the while catching glimpses of what kind of storm it was possible to work up, by watching killer touring bands including John Mayal's Bluesbreakers.

He caught them in Cardiff in 1965, and the finger work of a pretty-faced Eric Clapton knocked him out.

More than two decades later Andy would be head-hunted by Clapton to join his band for his 1992 Albert Hall gig, then for the recording on his ground-breaking MTV Unplugged disc.

Andy has taken a lot of calls like that over the years, from George Harrison, The Who, Roger Waters – and more. But before that success there were failures. Albeit teenaged ones.

It's a FACT

Dave Edmunds began his musical career playing with his piano-playing brother Geoff, who fronted the Heartbeats, playing every gig available in Cardiff and the Valleys. Then Dave struck out from the Heartbeats, forming the bass-and-drum heavy Raiders before Love Sculpture, solo success and Rockpile came knocking.

One Battle of the Bands at the Ritz in the mid 1960s saw Andy's crew pipped to victory by Eyes of Blue.

"And rightly so." he laughs. " They were better."

That outfit was fronted by Swansea R&B shouter Gary Pickford Hopkins. But unbloodied by that early setback, and, he says "too young to realise that we had a lot to learn," Andy formed Amen Corner with his brother-in-law Neil.

Setting off for London and soon picked up by Deram Records, their early tours saw the band sharing the bill with The Move, Pink Floyd, The Nice, The Outer Limits, Heir Apparent and Jimi Hendrix.

"Within six months of leaving school I was in London playing in places like the Speakeasy when the Stax tour was in town.

"It was in the days when you could play two or three gigs a night. I remember playing at 3am or 4am and Jimi Hendrix came in and got on stage. It's not my imagination. Honestly – it's written in one of the books about him. He said: 'I was in the Speakeasy playing with Amen Corner'."

Tom – the valleys hit man

Few pop singers have stayed nearly 50 years at the top, but one who has is Pontypridd's very own Tom 'The Voice' Jones.

Still rocking at the age of 73, Tom, who became Sir Tom in 2006, has had 36 Top 40 hits in the UK and 19 in the United States. That's no mean feat.

A young Tom Jones.

From his first British number one in 1965, It's Not Unusual, the hits have just kept coming, from Green Green Grass of Home to Delilah and What's New Pussycat. And they all remain favourites.

He has sold more than 100 million records and still sings in live concerts all over the world, including Las Vegas. It's all a long way from the valley dance halls and workingmen's clubs Tom used to play with his Welsh beat group, Tommy Scott and the Senators. They were appearing one night at the Top Hat at Cwmtillery when Tom was spotted by the legendary manager, Gordon Mills, who was himself from South Wales.

Soon Tom was playing at Caesars Palace and women were throwing their underwear and hotel key rooms at him on stage.

Tom retains a South Wales home, but now lives in Las Vegas and is still with Melinda, the girl he married in 1957.

Tom, who is also an OBE, plans to go on singing for as long as possible. "I can't see myself retiring," he said recently. "I hope I'll always be able to go out and do shows for as long as I live."

No doubt Tom's fans would hope so too!

Fair

ROLL up, roll up, for all the fun of the fair! Thousands of South Wales people did every summer in the 1950s and 1960s when the fairgrounds at Barry Island, Porthcawl and Aberavon Beach were in their heyday.

The smell of freshly made 'donuts', the prickly sensation of pink candy floss on the tongue, ice-cream and toffee apples, exciting amusement rides – the frenetic activity, all made a trip to the fair irresistible for old and young alike.

Coney Beach in Porthcawl is the older of the two. Its first permanent ride was put up in 1918, a Figure 8, that had been brought to Mumbles in Swansea by the American government to entertain their troops stationed in the town during the First World War.

At the end of the conflict it was moved to the site of an old seafront ballast tip at Porthcawl and to keep the American link this became known as Coney Beach as a tribute to the famous New York amusement park on Coney Island.

The move coincided with the decision to create a workers' holiday, the last week in July and the first week in August each year, which eventually became known as miners' fortnight. Porthcawl became a major holiday destination for the people of South Wales and the fairground's popularity grew and grew.

There had been small rides on the beach at Barry Island but when the town council built the promenade these were moved to a new permanent site in 1923. Later, in 1940, the fairground was enhanced by a new Scenic Railway ride which had a mile-long track and was the biggest wooden roller coaster ever built in the UK.

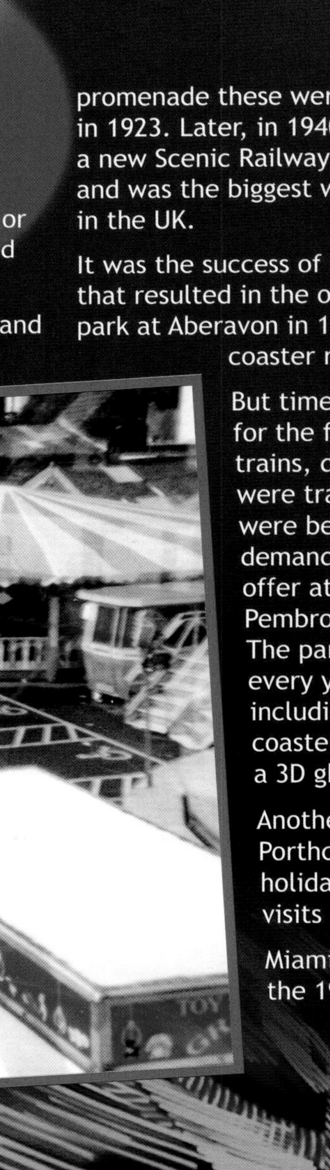

It was the success of Porthcawl and Barry fairgrounds that resulted in the opening of Miami Beach amusement park at Aberavon in 1963. It also had a popular roller coaster ride as its central attraction.

But time was already starting to run out for the fairgrounds. Helter-skelters, ghost trains, dodgems and merry-go-rounds were traditional rides, but holidaymakers were becoming more sophisticated and demanding greater thrills like those on offer at Oakwood Theme Park in Pembrokeshire which opened in 1987. The park is visited by 400,000 people every year and has the latest rides, including one of the biggest roller coasters in the world and a 3D ghost train.

Another problem for Barry and Porthcawl was the rise in package holidays abroad which meant fewer visits to traditional seaside resorts.

Miami Beach funfair lasted only until the 1980s when the site became

game

derelict and houses have now been built there. The future looks uncertain for Barry Island, despite its rides being updated and modernised in the 1980s and 1990s. The Scenic Railway was demolished after gales caused damage in 1973 and more recently the appalling summer weather of 2012 seriously hit visitor numbers.

Now hopes ride on a £70 million redevelopment package that will put the fairground under cover to escape our unpredictable summer weather.

The famous Figure 8 at Coney Beach was demolished in 1981 and the unique water chute, which dated back to 1932, went in 1995.

There are fears for the fairground's long-term future but it still has more than 20 attractions and has undergone extensive modernisation.

It would be a sad day for thousands of people across South Wales who have happy memories of summer holidays in Barry Island and Porthcawl if these fairgrounds were to operate their last ride.

Travelling fairs have been visiting South Wales for hundreds of years and the tradition is still as strong today.

Studts of Swansea, the John Collins and Deakins families, have all been prominent in bringing fairs to the valleys and towns of South Wales.

At the turn of the 20th Century the fairs would be made up of attractions like novelty mirrors, which would distort your image to make you appear thin or fat, strong man displays, freak shows and boxing challenges, as well as hoopla stalls.

Today the fairs are dominated by mechanised rides but there is still plenty of room for the traditional stalls.

South Wales's largest travelling fair is the Neath September Fair which is run by the Showman's Guild of Great Britain. The fair has its origins in a charter that was granted in 1280. It means the fair is the oldest in Wales.

Travelling fairs visit at any time of the year, but summer and bank holidays are most popular. A more recent innovation are winter fairs in Swansea and Cardiff.

Cardiff Winter Wonderland and Swansea Waterfront Wonderland are in effect "modern, traditional" travelling funfairs and each has the usual stalls and a Big Wheel you would expect to see at any fair.

They are perhaps adding their own 20th Century touch to the phrase 'all the fun of the fair.'

Town Times

High Street, Merthyr Tydfil, a hive of activity in the early 1900s.

The Esplanade at Porthcawl, 1920s.

Porthcawl postcard

Merthyr moments

Brecon Road, Merthyr, early 1900s.

Llanelli lookback

Llanelli Town Hall, 1950s.

A world first for Ammanford

It cannot lay claim to many of the world's firsts but, as JONATHAN ISAACS reveals, one did drive in to the sleepy Welsh town more than 50 years ago.

Invasion of the

It may have been just a humble bus but that first vehicle which started plying Ammanford's streets in December 1958 was to change the shape of bus travel forever, not just in South Wales but throughout the UK and countries all over the world.

For people in Ammanford who saw the double-decker on that cold winter's day more than half a century ago, it was a complete shock.

"There's a bus running in town without an engine!" was the first response. It did not even sound like a bus, instead of the growl of the Leyland and AEC vehicles the people of the town had long been used to, this vehicle seemed to purr.

The new bus also looked completely different.
It had a flat front and passengers boarded where the engine should have been. It also appeared strange from the rear, its top platform overhung the rest of the vehicle and there was a gap above a mounted compartment outside the main body which, of course, housed the vehicle's engine.

Children nicknamed it 'the funny bus' and revenue for the company that ran it, J James of Ammanford, rose as people flocked to see what it was like to ride inside. The bus, in J James's distinctive deep orange with a single maroon band livery, was a pre-production example of the exotically named Leyland Atlantean. There were six

A Leyland Atlantean leaves Ammanford for Neath.
Picture: G Lumb

Atlanteans

in all and three entered the fleets of J James, Glasgow Corporation and Wallasey Corporation that December.

But it was the Ammanford vehicle, registration number RTH 637 and given the fleet number 227 by J James, which was the first Atlantean in revenue earning service anywhere in the world.

Leyland had started experimenting with rear-engined double-deckers in 1952 and the first production Atlantean PDR1/1 was launched at the 1958 Commercial Motor Show. There were trials and tribulations but overall the concept was a huge success and by the time Atlantean production ended nearly 30 years later in 1986 no fewer than 15,000 had been built.

> **"The new bus looked completely different. It had a flat front and passengers boarded where the engine should have been."**

By this time others had followed Leyland's example, notably Daimler with its Fleetline and the Bristol VR, which became one of the most common sights in Swansea, Cardiff, Newport and other South Wales towns and villages from 1974.

Their success was down to the fact that they could be operated with the driver collecting fares as people boarded the bus which meant there was no need for a conductor. This made them cheaper to operate. Traditional double-deck buses were 'half-cabs', which meant the driver sitting in isolation in his cab at the front of the vehicle alongside the engine. Earlier buses had an open platform at the rear for passengers to board which was a Health and Safety inspector's nightmare as it meant passengers could jump off where they liked. Later models had platform doors which could be controlled by the driver but they still needed the expensive conductor.

One of the James company's Leyland Atlanteans about to set off for Ammanford from Neath General railway station, in the mid-1960s.

Even so, half-cabs continued to be made well into the 1960s. J James was well-pleased with its first Atlantean and bought another 12 over the next four years, a sizeable number in a fleet of just over 50 vehicles. They all had bodies by Metro-Cammell Weymann and Western Welsh, the biggest bus company in South Wales at the time, bought 66 similar machines in four batches between 1960 and 1962.

But other South Wales fleets were less impressed. Swansea-based South Wales Transport was a rigid user of half-cab double-deckers engined by AEC and continued buying them until 1967. It never bought an Atlantean, although it took on 12 from James's when it absorbed the company in 1962 and had a further four transferred from Western Welsh. Its first rear engined double-deckers bought new —Bristol VRs —did not arrive until 1976.

SWT certainly had no use for J James's Atlanteans when it took over the company in September 1962. Although it repainted them in its own livery they were eventually swapped, including that all important first vehicle, for more AEC Regents from Oxford.

Other South Wales fleets were also slow to take rear-engined buses, despite the economies they presented. Cardiff Corporation continued taking half-cabs with open doorways at the rear as late as 1966, although they swiftly made up for this with large batches of Fleetlines from 1967.

Newport Corporation did not start buying rear-engined buses until 1966, then bought nothing else. Its first were Alexander-bodied Atlanteans and these quickly introduced an exact fare system. This meant that instead of handing over a shilling (5p) to a friendly conductor for a 9d fare and receiving 3d change, you had to pay the right amount of money into a machine alongside the driver at the front of the bus — or lose your change.

Despite the large number of Atlanteans Western Welsh bought from 1960-62, the company went back to half-cabs and did not buy another rear-engined bus until much modified Northern Counties-bodied Atlanteans arrived in 1969. Perhaps some mechanical problems with its early examples put the company off, even so they all had full lives and some were still running in 1978.

Rhondda Transport, which had always bought Regents and continued to do so until 1966, did not receive its first Atlanteans, also bodied by Northern Counties, until 1968.

By then SWT, Western Welsh and Rhondda were suffering financial problems and all three became part of the National Bus Company which bought Bristol VRs for its fleets in South Wales. These were even more box-like than the Atlanteans because the rear engine compartment was covered and it was these ECW-bodied examples that became familiar sights from Gloucester in the east right across to Haverfordwest. They were basic and hardly passenger friendly so designers at Leyland got to work on a new bus which emerged as the Olympian in the early 1980s. SWT and National Welsh both bought some but they were never very numerous in South Wales.

In fact as far as double-deckers go, South Wales was becoming a bit of a desert. Passenger numbers continued to fall and cheaper single-deckers were adequate on most routes. The decline continued as the bus industry was privatised in 1986 and the number of double deckers has decreased with single deck vehicles predominating in South Wales. Newport and Cardiff however, have recently added to their combined total of 28 double deckers by buying new vehicles. Elsewhere the successors to that first Ammanford Atlantean go from strength to strength. Double-deckers, these days more commonly called twin-deck buses, rule in London and other major towns and cities in the UK. Arriva has even brought some back on it most popular North Wales routes. All have the same basic design as the Ammanford Atlantean, although advances have made them far more comfortable than the pioneering rear-engined buses of the late 1950s. Some even have luxurious leather seats.

Ammanford's Atlanteans on parade in the mid-1960s after the James fleet had been taken over by South Wales Transport.
Picture: Michael Rooum

"Passenger numbers were falling and as far as double-deckers went, South Wales was becoming a bit of a desert."

Despite these improvements, half-cabs with rear, open doorways were still operating in London until just a few years ago. They were the durable and reliable Routemaster but all were retired from regular passenger service in 2005. None ran on routes in South Wales. So while buses similar to the Atlantean continue to flourish today, the days of buses like the Routemaster are over. Or are they? Transport for London has recently ordered 600 examples of a new model — nicknamed the Borismaster after London Mayor Boris Johnson — to be delivered by 2016. They come complete with, you've guessed it, an open doorway at the rear!

The Western Welsh bus company also operated Leyland Atlantean double deckers.

Swansea was just one of the regular destinations for the James company's Ammanford-based Leyland Atlanteans.
Picture: Arnold Richardson

Days when Hannah Street had it all!

Hannah Street, Porth in the mid-1920s. Alongside, the industrial scene that generated the town's early prosperity.

HANNAH Street in Porth is today still one of the main shopping centres in the Rhondda but when this photograph was taken around 80 years' ago it was even more important.

For this was where everyone did the vast majority of their shopping and Hannah Street, particularly on Fridays and Saturdays, would have been buzzing. There was no need for people to go anywhere else.

Porth in the first half of the 19th Century was a rural idyll with just a few farms. All that changed with the advent of the coal industry and when the town's first pits were sunk in the 1840s the population rose dramatically.

As terraced homes were quickly built in Porth and on the surrounding hillsides, new shops became a priority and most were centred in Hannah Street. It became the hub of the town's life and anything a mining family might need could be found there. But it had more than shops, Salem Welsh Baptist Chapel was built in 1878-9 and in later years the latest films of the day were shown in Hannah Street's Central Cinema.

The street was in an ideal position for transport links. Porth lies at the gateway to the Rhondda Fawr and Rhondda Fach valleys and had good tram and later bus services. The railway station is even today just a few yards round the corner from Hannah Street.

It all meant a thriving, prosperous shopping centre which was the way things remained until the advent of supermarkets and out-of-town shopping centres from the late 1960s.

Hannah Street declined as shops began to close because of out-of-town competition. The chapel fell into disuse and was demolished in 1990 while the cinema became a bingo hall which itself closed in 2009. More recently the largest store, Woolworth's, also shut up shop for the last time when the parent company went out of business.

Nowadays Hannah Street appears to be dominated by takeaway restaurants whose silver-coloured roller blinds do nothing to enhance its appearance.

But the street's heart has not yet stopped beating. It has been modernised although there will be few who deny that much more needs to be done. Hannah Street has many independent, small retailers determined to see it survive.

Today you can still find butchers, greengrocers, bakers, florists, gift shops and shoe shops among the takeaways, banks and estate agents.

Hannah Street may have fewer shoppers, but with help it will be able to find a niche to keep it alive.

M. FREEDMAN
PAWNBROKER
CRIDLAND'S
BRIGGS
GUMMEYS
DUNNS

Signs
of the time

THEY are names that at some point will have been familiar to generations of consumers and they all had their individual colourful identity. Often this was emblazoned across the front of shops in a bid to lure us inside. Many of these signs and the products they advertised could be seen long after the corner shops they adorned or the products they promoted had vanished. Those seen here cover a plethora of products and are guaranteed to bring memories flooding back.

WILL'S's
"WILD WOODBINE"
CIGARETTES

DUNLOP STOCK
DUNLOP
The first tyre in the World

THE SMOKER'S MATCH
SWAN VESTAS
BRITISH MADE BY BRYANT & MAY.

AGENT FOR
B·S·A
BICYCLES

SOUTH Wales has had more than its fair share of disasters over the years, many of them related to coal mining. But there have been other tragedies too, both at sea, in the air and on the railways.

Disaster

Rescuers claw at the slurry-filled Pantglas school with bare hands.

The black terror of Aberfan

The one disaster that will always be indelibly etched on everyone's mind happened in the mining village of Aberfan on Friday October 21, 1966.

On that day the colliery tip above the village slid down the hillside, demolishing a farm and 20 houses on the way and smashing into Pantglas Junior School, filling some classrooms with thick mud and rubble 120ft deep.

It was the day before the half-term holiday, the school would have been empty the next day, and the children had just returned to their classrooms after singing All Things Bright and Beautiful in the morning assembly. They heard the roar of the landslide as it approached, the survivors said later it sounded as if a jet plane was about to crash – and 116 children, all under the age of 11, and 28 adults died.

A major rescue operation swung into action and desperate parents tore at the rubble with their bare hands in a frantic bid to reach trapped children.

strikes

. . . the children had only just finished singing All Things Bright and Beautiful

Some were dug out but no survivors were found after 11am that day.

Mining was always a dangerous occupation and there have been many deaths in the area's pits but thankfully none as serious as the two disasters that struck Senghenydd pit, north of Caerphilly, within 12 years in the early part of the 20th century.

On May 24, 1901, 81 men died when an explosion rocked the pit. But the lessons of that tragedy don't seem to have been learned because on October 14, 1913, the same mine was hit by another explosion and 439 of the 950 colliers died. It was the worst disaster in British mining industry and is believed to have been caused by an electrical spark igniting methane gas underground. Fines and compensation totalling just £24 were levied which means that each dead miner's life was valued at around 9p.

Death at the docks

Newport Docks hit the headlines in 1909 when 39 men lost their lives.

Only moments before the siren signalling the end of the working day on July 2, the walls of the new lock connecting the dock to open water collapsed, trapping or crushing scores of workers.

Cruel sea

Probably the worst sea disaster in the stormy history of the South Wales coast claimed the lives of 47 seamen including the eight strong crew of the Mumbles lifeboat.

The lifeboat had been launched to go to the aid of the stricken liberty ship Samtampa which was being driven ashore by 70mph gales at Sker Bay, Porthcawl.

The tragedy occurred on the night of Wednesday, April 23, 1947. The loss of the entire lifeboat crew ripped the heart out of the village of Mumbles. There were few villagers who didn't lose a relative or friend.

The upturned hull of the ill-fated lifeboat Edward Prince of Wales after the storm.

SKY HORROR

Families across South Wales were bereaved when what was then the worst disaster in aviation history occurred near Llandow aerodrome on March 12, 1950.

An Avro 689 Tudor V aircraft was bringing home a private party of rugby supporters from Dublin when it crashed on its final approach to Llandow. There were 78 passengers and five crew aboard and only three passengers survived. The plane had been chartered by a number of rugby clubs across South Wales so the whole region was affected by the tragedy in some way. After the crash the Court of Inquiry decided the probable cause was the way that the plane had been loaded.

Triumph had turned to tragedy as Wales had beaten Ireland that fateful weekend.

claimed rescuers

SOUTH WALES EVENING POST, April 24, 1947.

South Wales
Evening Post

LATE TOWN FINAL

No. 23,040 — THURSDAY, APRIL 24, 1947 — THREE-HALFPENCE

MUMBLES LIFEBOAT CREW SACRIFICE THEIR LIVES

Scene after night of tragedy

One appalling sea disaster after another near Porthcawl

BRAVE MEN DIED HERE—Mumbles life-boat and all that remains of the Samtampa, caught fast in the vicious belt of jagged rocks fringing Sker Bay, made a forlorn picture to-day which accentuated the poignancy of the tragedy which befell the crews. In the back-ground can be seen the boiling spume of the wind-lashed sea.

40 SEAMEN PERISH IN GALE

EIGHT GALLANT MEN

THE ill-fated Mumbles lifeboat-men who went out on their last trip last night were:

WILLIAM J. GAMMON, coxswain, of Thistle-boon.
W. NOEL, second coxswain, George Hotel, Mumbles.
G. DAVIES, mechanic, Lifeboat Cottage, Mumbles.
E. GRIFFIN, second mechanic, Mumbles-road, Norton.
W. THOMAS, bowman, Bracelet Bay.
D. SMITH, Hallbank, Mumbles.
R. THOMAS, George Bank, Mumbles.
W. HOWELLS, Clifton-terrace, Mumbles.

Wives and families who mourn

One life-boatman was to be married on Saturday

WITH few exceptions the crew of the lost Mumbles

He was a motor mechanic employed by a firm of engi-neers at the docks, and had

How the news spread in days when communication was far slower.

OF RUGBY TRIP PLANE

Pictures: South Wales Police Museum

Sightseers survey the stricken oil tanker Sea Empress. Below: tugs and helicopters played their part in the drama.

Day that the sea turned BLACK

The frailty of the South Wales coastal environment was thrust into the world spotlight in a shipping disaster that was to haunt the local headlines for many years, not least because of its impact on wildlife.

The Sea Empress was an oil tanker on its way to the Texaco oil refinery near Pembroke on February 15, 1996, when she ran aground at the entrance to Milford Haven harbour. Over the next seven days 72,000 tonnes of crude oil spilled into the sea and it could not have happened at a worst place for the environment.

This was Britain's only coastal national park and one of only three UK marine nature reserves. Thousands of sea birds died in the disaster and it took a year to remove the oil on shore. The cost of the clean up was estimated at £60 million and the effect on the economy and environment conservatively estimated at another £60 million.

Milford Haven Port Authority was fined a record £4 million and told to pay costs of £825,000. The Sea Empress was salvaged and repaired but banned from ever entering Milford Haven again.

Big **BANG** that woke a sleepy a seaport

At around 5am on Friday, February 2, 1951 Swansea had one of the loudest wake-up calls in its history.

A series of explosions shook people from their slumbers more than 10 miles away. It was the worst disaster ever to hit the city's docks. In the winter darkness, the oil tanker Atlantic Duchess, pictured below, carrying 12,000 tonnes of oil had blown up at No. 2 Jetty, Queen's Dock.

The horrific incident killed seven seamen and injured nearly as many firemen.

In an almost Titanic-style trip – it was the vessel's maiden voyage – the Atlantic Duchess had sailed from Abadan in the Persian Gulf with a Greek crew.

As the alarm was raised, Swansea fire engines headed for the docks to be joined later by crews from Morriston, Neath, Pontardawe and Pontarddulais. Tugs also used powerful water jets to cool the Duchess's hull and help keep it near the jetty. It took more than a day to bring the blaze under control and two weeks to recover the final body.

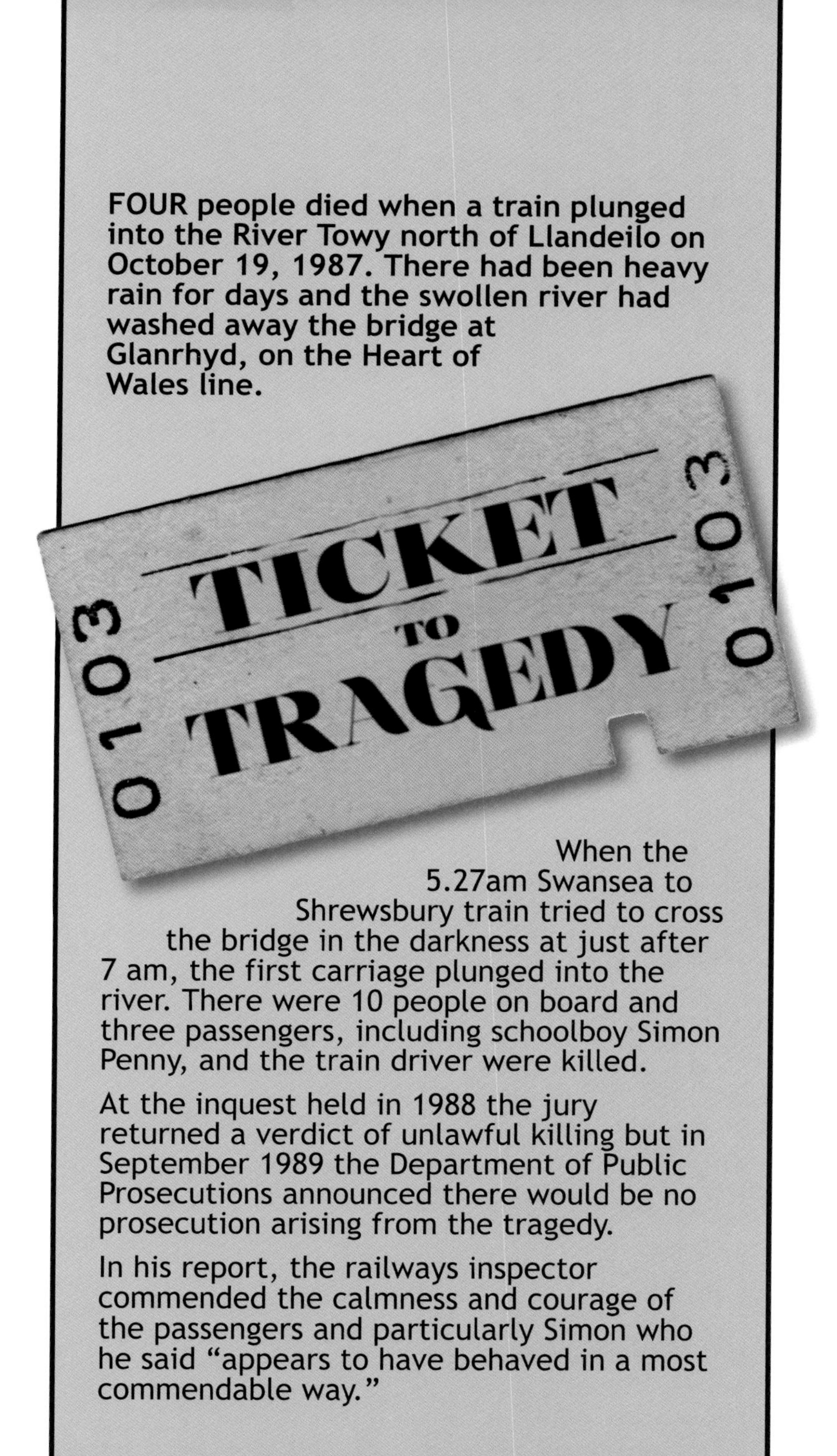

TICKET TO TRAGEDY

FOUR people died when a train plunged into the River Towy north of Llandeilo on October 19, 1987. There had been heavy rain for days and the swollen river had washed away the bridge at Glanrhyd, on the Heart of Wales line.

When the 5.27am Swansea to Shrewsbury train tried to cross the bridge in the darkness at just after 7 am, the first carriage plunged into the river. There were 10 people on board and three passengers, including schoolboy Simon Penny, and the train driver were killed.

At the inquest held in 1988 the jury returned a verdict of unlawful killing but in September 1989 the Department of Public Prosecutions announced there would be no prosecution arising from the tragedy.

In his report, the railways inspector commended the calmness and courage of the passengers and particularly Simon who he said "appears to have behaved in a most commendable way."

Tugs aid the Atlantic Duchess.

Cowboys and indians wasn't just

Imagine the scene. It's 1903 and the streets of Ebbw Vale, Aberdare or Neath are filled, not with steelworkers, miners or farmers wives out to do their weekly shopping, but with whooping cowboys and shrieking Indians, gaily but terrifyingly daubed in their war paint.

There is a smell of gunsmoke in the air, the thunder of horses hooves echo down the roadway. Buffalo Bill and his Wild West Show have come to town.

It's hard now, to know what Welsh men and women would have made of the spectacle. It was not just outside their experience, it was light years away. They may have read about cowboys, perhaps even seen pictures in the popular papers, but to meet them face to face? It must have been a mind-blowing experience.

William Cody came three times to Britain, firstly in 1887 to help celebrate Queen Victoria's Golden Jubilee. His visit was so successful that he returned four years later in 1891 and then again in 1902. The British, and the Welsh in particular, could not get enough of Buffalo Bill.

Cody was undoubtedly a man of action. By the age of 15 he was riding for the fabled Pony Express. By 1864 he was a scout for General Phil Sheridan and three years later had become a buffalo hunter for the Kansas Pacific railroad. It was said that he shot over 4,000 buffaloes in a two year period, which was how he got his name.

International fame came with a written report telling how he acted as a guide for the Grand Duke Alexis of Russia on his tour of the west. This was soon backed up by a lurid 'penny dreadful' novel, written by Ned Buntline, called Buffalo Bill, King Of The Border Men.

The legend that was Buffalo Bill.

PHIL CARRADICE recalls the days when a cowboy hero and his Red Indian pals made their mark across South Wales.

In 1883 Cody decided it was time to make a little money out of his experiences. He would, he thought, show people what the American West was really like and formed his famous Wild West show. He was not the first to form such a band, the original Wild West shows having begun in the 1840s. But he was the best.

When Cody was asked to come to Britain in 1887 he brought with him over 500 people - cowboys and Indians, back stage workers, grooms and so on. He also had 180 horses, 18 buffalo and numerous other animals including elks and Texas longhorn cattle.

Despite what many people believe, Sitting Bull - one of the victors over General Custer at the Battle of Little Bighorn in June 1876 - did not accompany him on this first trip to Britain. Sitting Bull did appear in the show in the USA in 1885 but did not travel across the Atlantic and by

Part of one of Buffalo Bill's colourful advertising posters.

a game on South Wales streets...

WHEN THE WILD WEST ROLLED IN

1890 he was dead. The famous Annie Oakley, sharpshooter and trick shot specialist was in the company and it was reported, she even shot a cigar out of the mouth of the German Kaiser who had come to help his grandmother celebrate her jubilee.

When Cody returned to Britain in 1891 he stayed for over 12 months and visited many different cities. Amongst them was Cardiff. He was clearly fond of the place as he made a six-day stopover, netting a cool £10,000 in the process. He set up camp in Sophia Gardens, creating an arena 175 yards long and 70 yards wide.

Here the people of Cardiff and the surrounding valleys could see Indian braves and their families resting outside their tepees and stare in wonder at the huge buffaloes that wandered peacefully around the park. A parade through the centre of Cardiff saw huge crowds thronging the roads and as a publicity exercise it was a dramatic success.

On the first day of the show over 20,000 spectators packed into Sophia Gardens. The next three days were just as popular and it was estimated that, overall, nearly 130,000 people came to watch Buffalo Bill and his showmen.

Cody made a return trip to the UK that lasted from 1902 to 1904. The show toured Wales for several months and visited places that included Aberdare, Abergavenny, Cardiff, Porthmadoc, Rhyl, Carmarthen and Pembroke Dock. In all Cody gave 333 performances during this visit. One of the highlights was an attack on the Deadwood Stage, Cody himself holding the reins and with local dignitaries — even, if he could persuade them, members of the royal family — inside the fast-moving stagecoach.

This was Buffalo Bill's last visit, however. Ill health and a series of financial misfortunes prevented him returning. He may have made considerable sums of money from his shows but the vast retinue of animals and performers cost a huge amount of money to maintain.

When he died in 1917, William Cody was virtually bankrupt but his position as one of the most famous showmen of the age — second only to the great Barnum - was assured.

He had many imitators, such as Texas Bill Shufflebottom and Bronco Billy, but, as the people of Cardiff and all of Wales would certainly have acknowledged, there was only ever one Buffalo Bill Cody and only one real Wild West show.

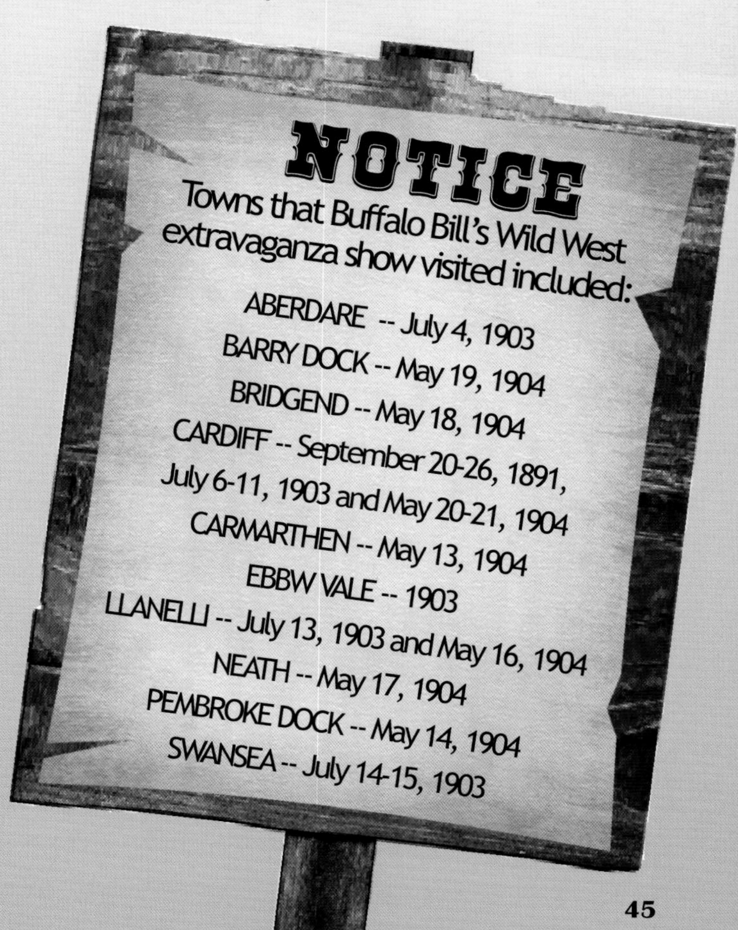

Forget Santa Claus and all his helpers at the North Pole, there was a time when Christmas joy was made in Swansea as DAVID ROBERTS recalls!

corgi Toy story

For nearly half a century a real life toy story was played out in Swansea amid scenes beyond the wildest dreams of even the most imaginative youngster.

Almost by accident the city became a mecca for many of the leading names in the manufacture of popular playthings. In huge, sprawling factories many hundreds of workers turned out almost everything you could think of. From typewriters to teddy bears and footballs to model vehicles. And at the height of this make-believe industriousness what could have been justifiably nicknamed Toy Town gave birth to one of the most successful toy ranges of the 20th Century - Corgi.

The combined production effort was on the kind of scale that would have left Santa and his little helpers in the shade. Companies like Louis Marx, Mettoy, Playcraft, Fisher Price, and Mattel were all linked to sprawling factory developments around Fforestfach and in later years, Skewen near Neath.

Strangely it wasn't peace at playtime, but the ravages of war that had first brought the factories and their occupants — toy companies who had turned their attention to boosting the war effort with the production of weapons and armaments.

Among these it was Mettoy who struck gold with the launch of the fantastically-detailed Corgi models in a bid to cash in on a lucrative market, dominated until that time, by Dinky Toys and Meccano.

Inside the sprawling Swansea factory that battled to satisfy the global demand for Corgi toys.

After the war Mettoy quickly returned to toy manufacturing, and by 1948 had started building a new, light, airy and worker friendly factory at Fforestfach with a host of modern production boosting features. It was officially opened on 2 April 1949, and was further extended to 200,000 sq. ft. at the beginning of 1952.

The increase in size allowed the installation of high-capacity injection-moulding machinery, which in turn enabled the company to move away from the manufacture of tinplate toys to those produced from plastic, in the process establishing strong export

The Batmobile, above, was the biggest selling Corgi die-cast model in the company's history.

It's a FACT

The name Corgi Toys was chosen by Philip Ullmann in honour of the company's new home, taken from the Welsh breed of dog, the Corgi, and the iconic Corgi dog logo branded the new range. The name was short and easy to remember, further aligning the range with their rival Dinky Toys.

markets. The late 1950s to mid-1960s saw an increase in the number of products offered by Mettoy. New ranges included the Wembley vinyl sports and play balls; Sunshine vinyl figures and Aurora plastic model kits. They also included Playcraft Railways, Vapour Trails model aircraft, Child Guidance Toys and Electric Highways the forerunner of the Champion electric-powered racing system. Mettoy also took over exclusive marketing of products manufactured by other companies, including the Bandbox radio and the Petite Typewriter.

The cornerstone of Mettoy's success and expansion however, was the Corgi range launched in 1956. The first six vehicles were British saloon cars, but the range expanded quickly. By the following year the range, growing at the rate of a model a month, included a number of larger vehicles, such as Bedford lorries and Mobilgas petrol tankers. In 1964 the Corgi Classics and Husky ranges were also introduced. The former, featuring models of veteran and vintage cars, was launched to celebrate Mettoy's 30th anniversary, while the latter was produced exclusively for the Woolworths chain.

In 1973 it acquired 48,000 sq. ft of additional space at Skewen, near Neath, for assembly and storage. The following year, a new Corgi production plant, one of the most modern die-casting foundries in the country, was built at Fforestfach. The Skewen warehouse was also expanded, as were production facilities for the Fisher Price range, the manufacture and distribution of which Mettoy had negotiated in 1971. Corgi turned an almost 30-year, world toy spotlight on Swansea. It seemed there was no stopping the popularity of the fantastically detailed model range. These new toy cars were such a huge hit because at the time they were the only toy cars on the market that included transparent plastic windows, they soon became known as 'the ones with the windows.'

Clouds of smoke billow from the factory during the 1969 fire.

Popular models

- James Bond's Aston Martin DB5
- Inspector Morse's Jaguar Mk II
- The Italian Job Minis
- Doctor Who's TARDIS and Daleks
- Basil Fawlty hitting his Austin 1100 Countryman with a branch
- Mr. Bean's Yellow Mini

In its first year of trading they sold an amazing 2.75 million cars, making it a clear leader of the British toy car industry. In 1966 Corgi won both the very first Queen's Award to Industry and the National Association Of Toy Retailers' Highest Standards Award, two prestigious awards.

Sales had rocketed, partly due to the overwhelming success of the James Bond Aston Martin DB5 and the Chitty Chitty Bang Bang cars, but sadly the bubble burst in March 1969 when a year's supply of models was destroyed by a huge blaze at the Fforestfach factory. It was a major setback, which lost retail confidence and cut the company's profits tremendously.

For a while Dinky Toys once again gained ground, but by 1971, the Swansea factory was back to full production again after major repairs costing over £1.3 million.

The Queen's Silver Jubilee model edition coach in 1977 was an instant best seller, along with another nostalgia model, Edward VII's coronation state coach of

Company that made its Marx

The Louis Marx toy company moved in to a new factory at Swansea Industrial Estate, Fforestfach, in September 1948. From there it produced a wide range of high quality, sought after toys but the factory was finally closed on January 2, 1981 after what can only be described as a rocky financial ride covering many years.

The company had a number of owners during this time and it was suggested that the reason for the eventual demise was that it had largely ignored the trend towards electronic toys in the early 1970s.

corgi

1901. But times were changing. In 1983 economic analysts said that decline was inevitable; children and adults had moved on to more sophisticated toys, others however did not agree; they believed if it had not been for the fire there would have been no problem. The company reformed as Corgi Toys Ltd in 1984 and focussed its attention on regaining the British toy company's confidence. Three years later Corgi turned to the export market for profits, soon distributing in Australia, Continental Europe and the United States. Shortly after this Corgi started the Collectors Club, which quickly gained worldwide membership.

In 1989 the company was taken over by Mattel, the worldwide toy manufacturing giant manufacturer which produced Barbie Dolls and Hot Wheels cars, and production was moved to Leicester.

Although Corgi has had many model car competitors ranging from Dinky Toys to Lledo, its name still endures with many of the children who played with those early models still coveting them and the Corgi name as dad's and granddads!

On the right Lines

The giant Tri-ang factory.

Merthyr Tydfil was another South Wales location which provided exciting playthings for generations of children around the world.

The massive Lines Brothers organisation brought the manufacture of its Tri-ang toys to a huge new factory in the town in 1948. The brand was another leader in the toy world and production began in earnest on items ranging from large scale pressed steel vans and lorries to Pedigree dolls prams, bicycles, scooters and much more. There was almost something for every tiny toy taste, but with children demanding ever more sophisticated playthings the company began to struggle in a highly competitive market. A rescue attempt failed and in 1978 the closure of the plant was announced. Workers battled for survival, occupying the factory and selling off its stock at bargain prices to eager buyers who flocked there.

Tri-ang

Mount Stuart Square, Cardiff in the mid-1920s.

Capital Creation

Cardiff city centre has changed dramatically since this rare photograph was taken in the mid-1920s. It shows the statue of the second Marquess of Bute in the distance at the bottom of St Mary's Street, close to the wall hiding the Glamorganshire Canal, near Mill Lane. The Great Western Hotel is centre left. The photograph was taken from the direction of the Great Western Railway's General Station, now of course, Cardiff Central.

In other words it lies behind the photographer. The approach is still there and is superficially similar to the one shown. Most of the buildings have now gone, with the exception of the Great Western Hotel. The statue of the second Marquess of Bute was moved to Callaghan Square some years ago in order to accommodate a new road alignment in this area which has changed the appearance of the locality significantly.

Emlyn

Emlyn Williams was president of the South Wales area of the National Union of Mineworkers from 1973 to his retirement in 1985, a period that ended in a desperate year-long struggle for existence which the miners eventually lost.

Stockily built with black hair, steely brown eyes and a voice that sounded like coal being shovelled into a bucket, Emlyn appeared a daunting character who you messed with at your peril. His was a multifaceted personality, he gave no quarter to his enemies but could be incredibly kind to those who showed him their loyalty and was like a father figure to his miners.

As far as Emlyn was concerned, the enemies were those who would do harm to the South Wales coalfield and its miners and in the first half of the 1980s that meant the government of Margaret Thatcher which was instigating a pit closure programme. He detested her and her policies which he said could almost be described as fascist.

He wondered why "no-one has risen up against this government" and went even further at the South Wales NUM conference in 1981.

“As real democrats, we have a responsibility to stop an oppressive government just as in the early 1930s the German trade unions had a responsibility to prevent the spread of Nazism,” he told the delegates. “We have a social responsibility to take extra-parliamentary action against Mrs Thatcher's government.”

Emlyn was convinced the government wanted to destroy the way of life in the South Wales valleys and closing the area's mines was one of its prime objectives. His defiance came from being a valley boy himself, a miner's son born in Aberdare in the early 1920s who followed his father down the local Bwllfa colliery at the age of 15.

Afan Valley miners — the evidence of another strenuous shift underground clear for all to see.

the Kremlin

THEY nicknamed him 'Emlyn the Kremlin' but as JONATHAN ISAACS reveals there was much more than communist style militancy to the man who led the South Wales miners through 12 of their most turbulent years.

He became a full-time trade union official in 1957 acting as miner's agent for collieries in the Rhondda, Cynon Valley and Merthyr Tydfil areas and was South Wales vice-president before being elected as president in 1973. He could have had a political career, he was certainly asked many times, but he believed his calling in life was to represent his members.

That did not stop him taking part in politics – he was a lifelong member of the Labour Party – and his skill as an orator livened up many a turgid debate at Wales Labour Party and Wales TUC conferences. When it came to speaking from the heart, he was unsurpassed but he was less successful at reading prepared speeches. During one presidential address at an area conference in Porthcawl he got lost halfway through, announced to delegates "Oh hell, I've gone wrong" and had to restart.

Coming from Aberdare his outlook on life was very much a valley one, and that included the male attitude to women. Like most valley men of his time, Emlyn believed a woman's place was in the home and he never changed. I remember during the 1984-5 strike going to NUM area headquarters in Pontypridd with other hacks – all male – for an update on how things were going. Suddenly a young female reporter walked in

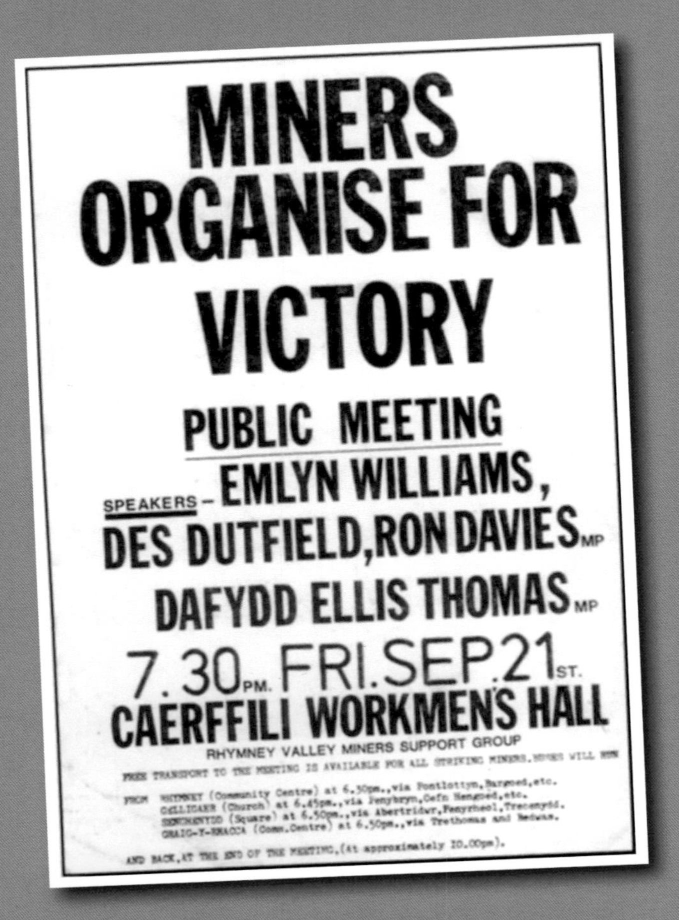

which shocked Emlyn. Not only was she a woman, she was also English and she compounded these deficiencies when she started asking hypothetical questions.

Emlyn's patience finally snapped: "How the hell do I know," he barked in reply to one of her 'what if' questions. "I'm not bloody clairvoyant."

The tale is an example of his sense of humour, but it was for the passion in his speeches that I most remember him, such as the one he made at a rally in Pontypridd during the year-long strike when he declared: "The South Wales NUM was born on this spot and we'll die here if necessary."

He made another memorable speech in 1976 calling for £100 a week for face-workers: "Why should men who risk their lives, who work hard, who produce a commodity essential to British industry not be paid accordingly?" he asked. "And if the answer is that society cannot afford it then my reply is that society must be changed so that it can afford it."

Many of the views expressed in his speeches could certainly be described as "militant" and he believed that industrial might was an essential component to safeguard the future of mining: "There must be a strike in support of the coalfield of South Wales" was a rallying call he made.

But Emlyn was also a pragmatist. It has to be remembered that there were 88,000 miners working for the National Coal Board in South Wales in the early 1960s and this was down to 20,000 by the time of the 1984-5 strike.There had been pit closures and job losses during his period as a full-time NUM official. The closures had been agreed by the union when pits became too dangerous to be worked or were running out of coal reserves.

Things were very different at the start of the 1980s. Joe Gormley retired as NUM national president in 1981 to be replaced by the militant Arthur Scargill. Emlyn and Joe Gormley hated each other with a passion and the national leader would not have expected an affectionate farewell from the South Wales president.

Pit points

- Mines started being sunk in 1850 and between then and 1911 the area's population shot up by 366,000 as people flocked to work in them.
- Striking miners fought hand to hand with police on Tuesday, November 10, 1910, in Tonypandy, Rhondda. Shop windows were damaged in the town and Home Secretary Winston Churchill sent in troops to quell the disturbances, which became known as The Tonypandy Riots.
- The worst mining disaster in the UK was at Senghenydd Colliery near Caerphilly on October 14, 1913, when 439 men lost their lives.
- The last deep mine in South Wales was Tower at Hirwaun which was sold to its miners in 1995. It employed 375 men and closed in 2008.
- Mining tragedies continue today. On 15 September, 2011, four miners died when an explosion ripped through Gleision Colliery drift mine at Pontardawe in the Swansea Valley. Three others managed to escape.

Miners at Dyffryn Rhondda Colliery, Port Talbot.

Emlyn did not disappoint: he declared it was good riddance to the man he always called Gormley, usually through gritted teeth, and added for good measure that there was no depth to which the national president would not plunge to further himself.

Relations improved somewhat with Scargill at the helm but they were always uneasy, to put them at their very best. The brash, in your face Scargill was simply not the South Wales NUM style, which had always been one of strength through unity, modesty and a sense of humour.

There were those who were suspicious of the new president, he talked the right talk over pit closures but did he have ulterior motives?

Initially the South Wales NUM rejected Scargill's strike call over the Thatcher government's pit closure programme but by the late winter of 1984 every miner in the area was on strike and one of the greatest union struggles of the twentieth century was underway.

In fact South Wales became the most solid area behind the strike, no fewer than 21 of the 28 British pits still completely free of strike breakers in December 1984 were in the area's coalfield. But it was a struggle they could not win and under Emlyn's leadership it was decided to return to work without a settlement in March 1985.

Police officers on duty at Port Talbot Steelworks during the miners' strike.

It was a crushing defeat that set the South Wales coalfield on the short road to oblivion.

Shortly after the return to work, Emlyn retired to Cwmbach in the Cynon Valley, that jet black hair now mostly grey and those piercing eyes hidden by glasses. By the time he died in July 1995 aged 74, there was just one deep mine left. But there was nothing he nor anyone else could have done that would have made any difference.

The South Wales NUM, and its predecessor the South Wales Miners' Federation – nicknamed 'The Fed' – were fortunate in their leaders throughout the 20th Century. Some, including Arthur Horner and Will Paynter, went on to become national leaders of their union; Jim Griffiths of Llanelli became the first Secretary of State for Wales.

All were greatly respected leaders and honourable men.

Emlyn Williams richly deserves his place among them.

It's a FACT

Swansea suffered a yellow fever outbreak in 1865 when a copper ore cargo infested by infected mosquitos from Cuba docked in the town's port. A total of 27 people became ill and 15 died in the only case of the sickness on the British mainland.

Opportunity

Hughie Green

Television screens have been swamped by talent shows in recent years and in doing so provided a route to stardom for more than one young South Wales hopeful.

TV talent shows are nothing new as DAVID ROBERTS discovers during a chat with one of their most popular early winners.

But forget the X-factor, Britain's Got Talent or the Voice, for they are all simply following in the footsteps of the daddy of them all . . . ITV's Opportunity Knocks.

And when, in August 1965, the show's famous presenter Hughie Green uttered the ubiquitous words:

Some popular 21st Century TV Talent Shows.

"Tonight folks, Opportunity Knocks for Allun Davies, from Neath in South Wales," it certainly did.

For fresh-faced contestant Allun, a Co-operative bakery roundsman by day, the show turned the spotlight on his wonderful tenor voice. When the 23-year-old broke into the lyrics of the Richard Tauber song, 'Girls were made to love and kiss,' he wowed not just the young girls, but their mums too . . . and by the million. Better still they put pen to postcard and voted for him week after week. Allun was the first, and for a long time, longest running winner on the talent show that paved the way for all the others. He won for seven consecutive weeks, and wowed audiences once more in an all-winners show.

He even topped that by winning a special Opportunity Knocks show where the top two artists – Brenda Marsh was the other – joined the Great Britain team of Marty Wilde, Wayne Fontana and Friday Brown for a European song contest at Knokke in Belgium. Returning to his daily bakery round was like bread of

knocked for the baker boy from Neath

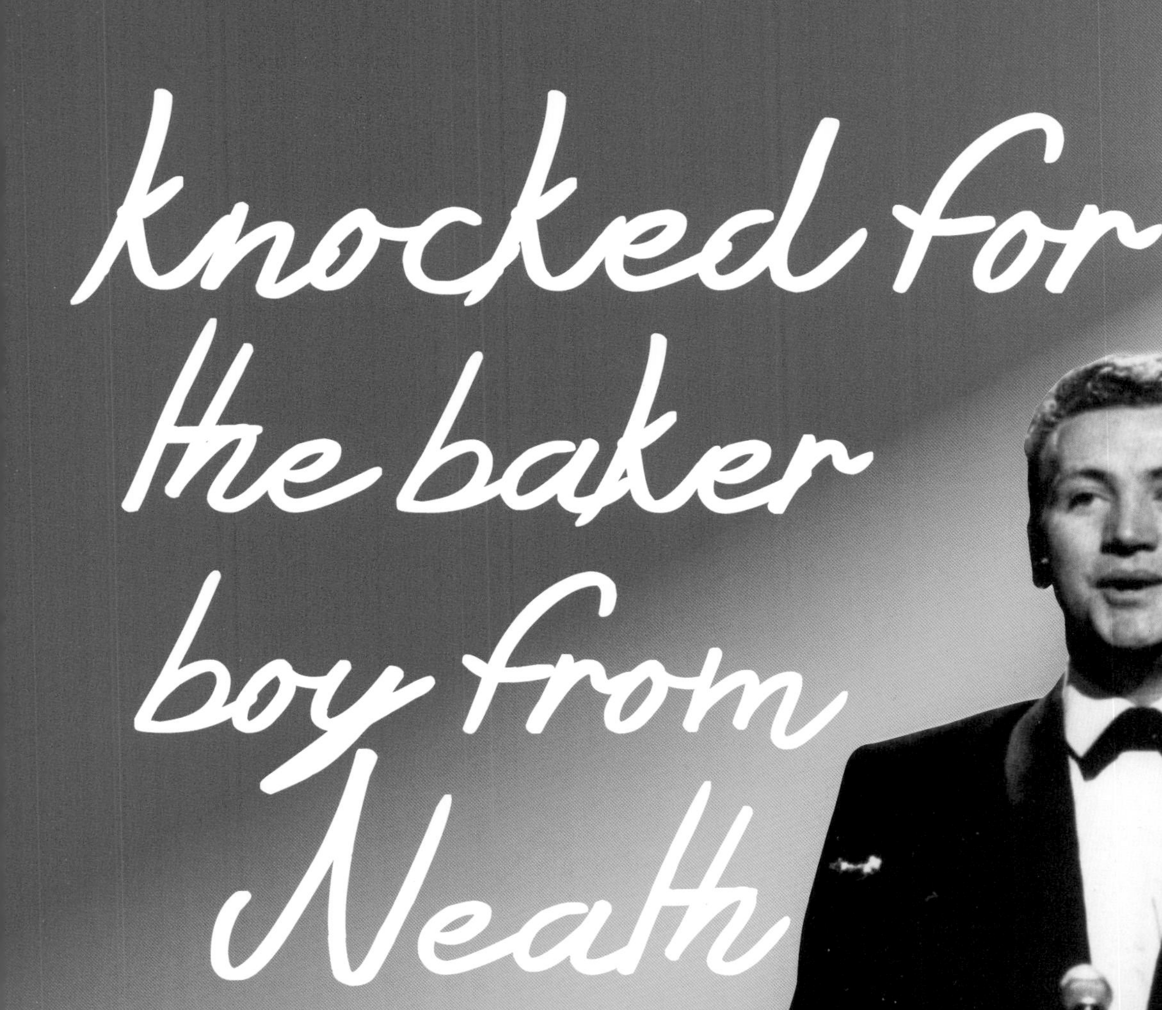

Heaven for Allun. "My round was a really big one that took me all over Neath and I think most of my customers were voting for me. When I went back to work on a Monday it was amazing. Many of them would stop me and play back my performance on portable tape recorders," said Allun.

"Walking through the streets of Neath after a show was marvellous. I was instantly recognised. Everyone wanted my autograph. On one occasion the town's Woolworths store ground to a halt as all the staff mobbed me.

"After you appeared on the Saturday you had to wait until mid-week before you had a telegram telling you that you'd won and that's when you began making arrangements with the orchestra on what you were going to sing that week. Often I would be out delivering and my cousin would have to come and find me to tell me the news and that I had to phone them right away.

"I had some wonderful telegrams when I was on the show including a lovely one from Shirley Bassey.

"I still have people come up to me in the street all these years after the show. They don't just remember me, they can even remember the songs I sung so I must have created a very favourable impression."

The events of those heady, distant days remain crystal clear for Allun even though he has now retired. Like the day he visited the town's Metal Box factory and Red Dragon Relays TV and radio company to be mobbed by many of his young, female fans. The girls from the David S Smith cardboard factory were all voting for him and he paid a visit there too. Whenever he could he took the time to visit his local fans and thank them for their support.
The very first show sticks in his mind too. " I remember we travelled up on the train the day

before and stayed in a hotel near the ABC Theatre, Didsbury where the show was recorded. All the artists stayed in the same hotel and there was a lovely atmosphere there. The TV company would send chauffeur driven cars to take us to rehearsals in the morning. There was a full orchestra in those days. Following a dress rehearsal the show was filmed before a live audience in the afternoon for broadcast that night at 6pm.

It's a FACT

The BBC rival to Opportunity Knocks — New Faces — was the first TV show to decide its winner by using the now-standard method of a telephone vote.

Allun's success saw offers of work flooding in and for him it marked a turning point. He gave up his delivery job and began singing full time, a move he has never regretted. He won a recording contract with EMI on the Parlophone label and brought out an EP. Hughie Green also invited him to appear on his other popular television show Double Your Money, where he sang viewers requests.

"I went on tour around the ABC theatre circuit with Hughie Green and other successful acts from the show before doing summer seasons, concert work and cabaret," he said.

"I had always loved singing. It was something I had been doing since I was 14 and my success gave me an opportunity to carry on doing that. I met some wonderful people and worked with many of the country's leading artists.

"I like to think that in a way I took good singing to the masses. In my time, I've sung everything from Nessun

"...and I mean that most sincerely, folks."

Games we used to play

Dominoes

Draughts

Jackstones

Skipping

Dorma to Spanish Eyes. You could call it education through singing."

Education certainly played a big part in the years that followed for Allun. He tutored many singers and helped their progress. Among them Mike Sterling who won the much later New Faces TV talent show and went on to play many leading West End and touring show roles.

People achieve success far quicker today. They come and go, but Allun Davies is justifiably proud of a long and successful career that saw him work with so many top entertainers all over the UK.

"The greatest delight I had through my singing career was meeting Joan Hammond and Anne Ziegler.
The result was friendships that endured until they sadly died. You can never be sure of who you will come across in your career and these were indeed two of our greatest singers. That was a real privilege.

"Today, TV talent shows are far different. They have a global audience and anyone lucky enough to appear on one of the shows can be sure that their performance will be witnessed by millions. For anyone who has ever dreamed of becoming a star they are a must."

Allun Davies, at 71, still with fond memories of the day when Opportunity Knocked.

— indoors and out

Snakes and Ladders

Marbles

Hopscotch

Cities make

Beautiful Roath Park, Cardiff, is regarded as one of the most important late-Victorian parks in Wales. And the jewel in its crown is the magnificent lake at its heart.

Cardiff crowds enjoy leisure time at Roath

Opened on June 20, 1894, it was built to create more recreational space in Cardiff when the city's population boomed in the wake of the coal industry. Its centrepiece is the lake, more than a mile round.

The park itself cost £55,000 and was formally opened by the Earl of Dumfries, eldest son of the third Marquess of Bute. Its creation followed 12 years of negotiations, between 1875 and 1887, involving Cardiff Corporation and various landowners including the Marquess of Bute and Lord Tredegar.

Much of the park, particularly where the lake and recreation ground are located, was established on low-lying and poorly drained land through which the Roath Brook or Nant Llechau ran. So it is not surprising that the construction involved a large amount of work in levelling, draining and road development.

The park was laid out and designed from 1889 by Cardiff Corporation's engineer, William Harpur, and the council's head gardener, William Pettigrew.

Historically, Roath Park and its lake fell within the ecclesiastical parish of Llanishen; it was only the 23-acre recreation ground which was located in Roath parish.

The Pleasure Garden, lying between Fairoak Road and Alder Road, was completed in April 1894 with the Wild Garden area, at the north end of the lake, opened in May 1896. The ornamental lake, covering 29 acres, dominated the layout which comprised winding paths, boat house, landing stage, bathing platform, bandstand, botanic gardens, pleasure gardens and recreation ground.

Down the years some features have been lost. Among them the bandstand, which was built in 1903, aquarium, the original propagating house and boat house as well as the rockery. In all its essentials, however, the park retains much of its internal layout such as paths and many of its trees still in existence as are the Victorian and Edwardian villa residences on Lake Road East and Lake Road West. The park remains very popular. Roath

Newport hotspot

The City of Newport too, has long laid claim to a watery masterpiece. It is the magnificent lake within the grounds of Tredegar House, seen above.

In its time it has proved popular with boating enthusiasts – both models and the real thing – fishermen and those who simply enjoy a stroll around its banks.

a splash!

Water-based recreation has played a big part in the lives of South Wales people as JEFF CHILDS reveals.

Two views of Roath lake.

Picture: Malcolm Ranson

Park Lake covers 29 acres and lies to the south of the main area of the park. It takes up almost the width of the park and is dammed at its southern end by a large, straight, stone embankment.

The lake has stone-edged sides except on the south while at its northern end are five small islands planted mainly with mixed deciduous trees, including copper beeches, pines and rhododendrons.

It is populated by numerous ducks and other waterfowl and is also used for fishing and boating, the landing stage and boat houses being located at the south-west end of the lake.

The lake's Scott Memorial Lighthouse commemorates the ill-fated expedition of Captain Robert Scott from Cardiff to the South Pole in 1910.

It comprises a tall, clock tower lighthouse, erected in 1915. The white painted cylindrical structure is surmounted by a square clock tower and balcony with a weather vane resembling Scott's ship on top.

Sailing

Swans and sailing boats have long shared the delights of Brynmill Lake, Swansea as the pictures here show. They cover many decades, but all share the same theme of relaxation and enjoyment.

along in Swansea

Brynmill Lake has long provided an entertaining distraction for Swansea people. It remains the glorious centrepiece to beautiful Brynmill Park – the city's first informal public park.

The lake preceeded the park. It originated as an early, but unsuccessful reservoir built by the Swansea Waterworks Company in 1837. The five and a half million gallon capacity reservoir was intended to supply the needs of the locality, but it was situated at too low a level to work successfully.

In 1852 the local Boards of Health bought Swansea Water Works Company and the reservoir for £25,250. The area ceased to be a water supply for the city and in 1871 the land surrounding the reservoir came under Swansea Corporation control. It had been informally used for picnicking since the 1840s and was then developed as a formal park with the initial phases of construction taking place in the 1870s. By 1913 the area had been officially named Brynmill Park. The remnants of the reservoir were used for fishing and in the 1950s a large motor boat took people on trips around the lake.

In 2006, The Heritage Lottery Fund awarded a grant for the restoration of Brynmill Park and work started on refurbishment in 2007 during which, volunteers from Swansea University made valuable contributions to the redevelopment of the lake and the introduction of nesting areas for birds. They constructed a floating Island and also helped with planting around the lakeside.

Daring escapes in times of war and peace are the stuff of blockbuster movies and gripping yarns. One of the most fascinating took place in the heart of South Wales as HERBERT WILLIAMS recalls . . .

S.S. Men In Mass Jail Tunnel Getaway

70 OUT—28 BACK

"Herald" Reporter, VALE OF GLAMORGAN, Sunday Night

SEVENTY Nazi S.S. men, soldiers, sailors and airmen broke out of a Bridgend camp this morning.

They made the getaway at 4 a.m. through a tunnel under three barbed-wire barriers as guards patrolled above them.

Throughout to-day planes and hundreds of armed soldiers scoured South Wales and the West Country. Late to-night 42 of the prisoners were still at large. Some of them may be armed.

Forest Cordon

TOKYO'S HEART IS NOW ASHES

From CHARLES LAMBERT "Herald" Reporter, Washington, Sunday.

THE heart of Tokyo has been burned to ashes and smouldering ruin. A million people are homeless.

About 15 square miles of factories, offices and houses—with the small-scale domestic industry that was carried on in the larger Japanese homes—have been utterly destroyed by the myriad showers of incendiaries dropped by 300 Super-Fortresses in Friday's raid.

Shortening War

Freed By Russians—Returning

It was the escape that was almost bound to happen.

Forget the films and forget the fiction too — when it comes to great escapes South Wales can trump them all with a tale that couldn't be truer, ranking alongside Colditz and all the rest.

Yet despite that, the episode is one of the most forgotten events of the Second World War even though it spread fear and panic across the region.

There are many stories frequently told about British prisoners of war and their bravery and daring bids for freedom, but the tables were turned in March 1945 when 67 German prisoners of war went on the run — from Bridgend!

Their daring escape from Island Farm camp was the largest German break-out during hostilities and to this day ranks as the biggest prison escape attempt in the UK.

The mass bid for freedom led to a huge manhunt involving thousands of troops, policemen and civilians. Even Scouts and Girl Guides together with schoolchildren joined in the chase.

The days after the event brought with them incidents of horror and humanity, bravery and bravado, folly and in all of the cases failure. That was without the official questions as to how the huge dash for freedom was allowed to happen in the first place.

Perhaps it is not difficult to begin imagining why. Island Farm camp began life as a series of huts built for women munitions factory workers at Bridgend but few liked the idea of living away from home and the camp fell into disuse. Later it became a temporary base for American GIs in the build up to D-Day, but after the invasion of Europe the camp once again fell empty. With the successful Allied advance across Europe there was a rapid rise in the number of German prisoners being taken and Island Farm soon took on another, far different role — it became a prisoner of war camp.

The camp wasn't quite ready for its important new role when the new charges began arriving there towards the end of 1944. And as bizarre as it may seem now, the prisoners were even employed in adapting the huts and putting up the barbed wire entanglements which familiarised themselves not only with the locality, but more importantly the camp defences. By now the war was almost over and it might be thought that there was little point in escaping back to a country that was all but in ruins. That wasn't the thinking behind many of the Germans involved however.

FROM HUT 9

Panic and fear after wartime break-out

Their arrival was meant to be top secret. But this was Bridgend and everyone knew everyone else's business, even in wartime. Word spread like wildfire that hordes of grey uniformed Nazis were pouring out onto the platform at the town's station. It was enough to draw scores of onlookers there and it slowly dawned on all concerned that these were no ordinary troops. They were in fact high ranking officers who had dedicated their lives to the Fuhrer. Far from being defeated and dispirited they were fanatical and determined never to give in.

They were certainly of a different calibre to the camp guards. They were tall, upright and imposing. Their guards meanwhile were in the main either old men or soldiers intent on sitting out the war in as much comfort as possible even though their role was to secure as many as 1,500 prisoners.

An escape attempt was bound to come. One tunnel was discovered by the guards in January 1945 but the prisoners did not give in. On the night of May 10, 1945, 66 prisoners made their bid for freedom through a second tunnel leading from the floor of Hut Nine to a spot outside the barbed wire fence. The tunnel stretched for more than 60 feet and when investigations were carried out it was discovered that the earth from the excavation had been taken out and hidden behind a partition built by the prisoners especially to conceal it. Eleven escapees were quickly caught, one after being shot and wounded by a guard. Road blocks and army patrols were immediately established across the surrounding area but many of the prisoners were already well away from Bridgend. In groups of three, they were equipped with basic maps and compasses and most of them had supplies of food pilfered from the camp food store.

Some prisoners were apprehended before they had gone 10 miles; some found hiding in nearby woods with little idea where to go or what to do next. Others managed to get as far as Birmingham and Southampton before they were hauled in by the police or army. Not one succeeded in his bid for freedom – and Germany.

From the moment the first man emerged from the tunnel until the last was caught approximately a week had elapsed. The last group were caught in the Swansea Valley, tired and hungry and with very little idea where they were.

Island Farm prisoner of war camp closed in 1948, three years after the end of the war. By then,the men it held were allowed considerably more freedom than those involved in the Welsh Great Escape.
Several forged friendships and even found wives locally and never did head home.

The huts of Island Farm have now virtually disappeared although, several years ago, the discovery of wall paintings made by the prisoners did bring the escape back into the limelight for a brief period. Today Hut 9 is the sole survivor of the camp buildings. A small number of people passionately try to keep the memory alive and occasionally it is open to the public.

MUDDY

It's a trial even for a saint — St David that is

MARCH 1 is as good a date as any to host a special Welsh event - and the St David's Day Trial can certainly be classed as that.

ROGER GALE recalls one of South Wales's most successful motoring events — the St David's Motorcycle Trial organised by Neath Motor Club since the 1940s. It has been staged in and around the town, and the scenic Neath and Afan valleys attracting some of the world's greatest riders.

The event — for solo motorcycles, and occasionally also sidecar outfits — began in those far off days as a 'club' occasion for local riders, held on a date near to March 1st, the traditional date on which Wales celebrates its Patron Saint, and thus it was that the event took the name St Davids Trial.

The first competition was won by Thomas Hector Edwards, then of Neath town, riding his OK Supreme motorcycle. Hector — or T.H.E. as he was known — was a notable local rider of the time, a resolute supporter of Neath Motor Club, and indeed he became an honoured life member of the NMC in his later years.

The reputation and status of the St David's rapidly improved, and thanks to the efforts of the club and its members — led by John Macnulty, a club and Auto Cycle Union official — it became a National event, by 1950 firmly established in the motorcycle calendar, attracting riders from throughout the country.

The event then took in a 50 to 80 mile on and off road route, with 'observed' sections at intervals along the course.

The method of penalty — as it is today — was that riders collected marks against them for every time they had to put a foot down to the ground, or failed to complete a section, the rider with least penalties at the finish adjudged the winner. Various classes allowed riders of different abilities to compete, though the overall winner was naturally the most accomplished.

As the British motorcycle industry developed into a major force during the years from 1950 to 1965 both motorcycles and riders from this country filled the entry lists, and the motorcycle industry supported the St David's well, with KLG Spark Plugs, Dunlop Tyres and Reynolds Chains, just a few of the famous manufacturers involved — success on this and other major trials were a good advert for the reliability and performance of British bikes, and success always sold motorcycles!

The 'competition' motorcycle of those days was only marginally different to road bikes on general sale, many riders using one bike for trials and scrambles, as well as riding to and from the events, and using the machine for personal transport during the working week! With the event now called the St David's Reliability Trial, the major manufacturers such as BSA, Royal Enfield, and AJS to name but a few, used success in it to good effect in the adverts in the motorcycle magazines of the time.

The golden age of the British motorcycle industry and the National St David's Reliability Trial went hand in hand, winners making up a who's who of the era. They included eight times winner Sammy Miller — he missed out on a possible ninth win in 1966 as he had to be in Ireland for his father's funeral — on his famed Ariel 500 and in later years a Bultaco 250. Others were Gordon Jackson on a 350 AJS, trial and scrambler, Jeff Smith on a BSA 250 and Johnny Brittain on his Royal Enfield 350.

Heavyweight four stroke single cylinder machines had been favoured until the 1960s, but with Sammy Miller joining Bultaco as a works rider in 1965 the scene changed. Lightweight bikes were more effective and the

A competitor tackles the tough terrain of a typical St David's trial.

HELL!
20

old traditional sections such as ‘Keenans Clanger’ in the Neath Vale, the ‘Ladies Walk’ above Briton Ferry Library, and ‘Alex’s Horror’ at Penscynor were no longer difficult enough. With the arrival of the Spanish lightweight bikes from Bultaco, Ossa, and Montesa the course was changed from a long 50 mile route, to a closed off road circuit with multiple laps. This did away with the need to use land that was owned by perhaps 20 farmers, thus simplifying organisation and planning. A base in the Tonmawr region was used for around 10 years from the 1980s, the route crossing the mountain to Melyn Court near Resolven, and thereafter the Trial returned to the Neath Valley at Ynysygerwn, the Lletty Rafel Farm, then and now a wonderful home for the long-running competition, with the permission of Mr Richards, the landowner.

It's a FACT

Cardiff's first motorbuses ran in 1920 but its first trolley buses did not arrive until 1942. The last trolley bus ran in the city in 1970 and Cardiff 's fleet was unusual because it also had single-deck vehicles to get under a railway bridge at Bute Road.

The event has also enjoyed civic support, traditionally flagged away by the Mayor of Neath, one notable occasion that of 1959, a year in which the club also made Fred Rist – an expert racer and trials rider who ran a successful motorcycle dealership in Windsor Road – a life member of Neath Motor Club.

The Mayor, Alderman Howard Davies, criticised the ‘new’ speed limits, saying: “They are as much use nowadays as the old red flag system!” continuing to entreat NMC members to lobby their MPs for road tax to be used for better road building and repair – some things clearly never change! The St David’s Trial began its life in the days of rigid framed motorcycles, went on

A St David's Trial competitor gets a critical eye from Mayor of Neath Alderman Howard Davies and an event official.

through the era of the shock absorber and swinging arm suspension heavyweight bikes with big single cylinder engines, and on to the modern mono-shock sprung, water cooled engined, lightweights and those machine changes dictated changes to the course.

The rocky stream beds gave way to huge climbs over massive rock piles, near vertical hills, and far more technically challenging terrain for the new riders such as Welsh ace Steve Saunders and British and World Champion Dougie Lampkin, their control and agility on the new competition bikes amazing to witness.

With new riding talent constantly surfacing — like Graham Jarvis on his Sherco machine, who last won the Neath trial in 2006, along with the British National Trials Championship — there is a lot more to come.

Through it all the St David's has retained its position as a leading event in the British Trials Championship. The local trial run by Neath Motor Club has survived through six decades due solely to the dedication and enthusiasm of the various clerks of the course and volunteer officials from NMC, fellow motorcyclists and supporters. To this day the club has a strong and active membership, and surely a great future to add to an illustrious past.

I started my lifelong motor sport association observing on the St David's as a schoolboy, way back in the early 1960s, and still attend today, older if not wiser! I am indebted to John Victor for his remarkable insight into the history of this equally remarkable event. John competed as a rider for many years, his first St David's in 1964 on a 250 Royal Enfield, and he was clerk of the course on the St David's in 1978, indeed still riding today on a pristine DOT machine and an equally good HJH trials motorcycle, one of the machines built in the Canalside factory in Neath from 1954 to 1956.

The rugged sections of the St David's motorcycle trial have always provided the toughest of tests for rider and machine. Here, a competitor takes on the challenge of the rocky bed of a rushing mountainside stream.

ROARING

DAVID ROBERTS gets into gear to recall the days when the eyes of the world were focused on the little village with a big beach.

A tiny West Wales village might not, on first glimpse at least, seem the kind of place you would expect to be tagged as doing more than most places to put the roar in the roaring 20s.

But the achievements of the adventurous few who attempted to push the boundaries of speed further and further in the years around that frantic decade put such a statement beyond doubt. Cast an eye over the nine-mile stretch of sand carried into the tiny village streets of Pendine when the wind blows in from a stormy sea and the view is one of emptiness. In the 1920s and 30s it was different and the same view would be filled with thousands upon thousands of spectators for one high speed chase or another. It had all started in the early 1900s when the sands were used as a venue for car and motorcycle races. From 1922 the annual Welsh TT motorcycle event was held on the famous sands.

The firm flat surface of the beach created a race track that was straighter and smoother than many major roads of the time and the

A group of motorcycling enthusiasts at an event at Pendine Sands in 1947.

PUTTING THE ROAR INTO THE TWENTIES

Motor Cycle magazine described the sands as 'the finest natural speedway imaginable'. They weren't far wrong.

In the 1920s it became clear that roads and race tracks were no longer adequate venues for attempts on the world land speed record. As record-breaking speeds approached 150 mph the requirements for acceleration to top speed before the measured mile and safe braking distance afterwards meant that a smooth, flat, straight surface of at least 5 miles in length was needed. Pendine ticked all the boxes.

Malcolm Campbell before one of his record bids.

The first person to officially use Pendine Sands for a world land speed record attempt was Malcolm Campbell. It was a bid for supremacy in the world of speed that met with success. For on September 25, 1924 he set a world land speed record of 146.16 mph in his Sunbeam 350HP car that he had named Bluebird.

Four other record-breaking runs were made in the years between 1924 and 1927; two more by Campbell, and two by legendary Welsh speedster JG Parry-Thomas in his car Babs.

The 150 mph barrier was decisively broken, and Campbell raised the record to 174.22 mph

The glorious sweep of Pendine Sands.

in February 1927 with his second Bluebird. On March 3, the same year Parry-Thomas attempted to beat Campbell's record.

On his final run, while travelling at 170 mph the car crashed. It was said at the time that the exposed drive chain broke and partially decapitated Thomas. Babs went out of control and rolled over making Parry-Thomas the first driver to be killed in a world land speed record attempt. Parry-Thomas's car was buried in the sand dunes near the village of Pendine after his accident. In 1969 Owen Wyn Owen, an engineering lecturer from Bangor Technical College, received permission to excavate Babs which he spent the next 16 years restoring. The car can usually be seen on display at the Museum of Speed in Pendine village during the summer months. One further attempt at the land Speed Record was made on Pendine sands later in 1927 by Forresti in Djelmo.

In June 2000 Don Wales, grandson of Malcolm Campbell and nephew of Donald Campbell, set the United Kingdom electric land speed record at Pendine in Bluebird Electric 2, achieving a speed of 137 mph.

AIRBORNE AT PENDINE – THE FLYING *Sweethearts*

It wasn't just land-based records that were made and broken at Pendine. On one occasion in 1933 it was the world of aviation that captured the imagination of the public and brought them in their droves to tiny Pendine.

Amy Johnson was already a world famous pilot when she arrived at Pendine on Monday July 3, 1933. Amy and Scottish aviator Jim Mollison were known as the flying sweethearts and they hoped to cross the Atlantic as part of a bid for the world long distance flying record.

Amy, shot to fame in 1930 when she became the first woman to fly solo from Britain to Australia.

Jim too was an experienced pilot and in 1932 had become the first person to fly solo across the Atlantic in a westerly direction.

Seafarer surrounded by thousands of well-wishers on the sands at Pendine. Inset: Amy Johnson shares a smile with a photographer.

The couple chose Pendine in Carmarthen Bay for departure to America because the nine mile stretch of firm golden sand was a natural runway.

Seafarer's arrival at Pendine caused a huge stir and around 10,000 people descended on the village to catch a glimpse of the celebrities.

Day after day the couple checked weather reports to determine what conditions were like out in the Atlantic, but while the sun shone on Pendine the winds were too strong hundreds of miles out to sea.

The couple passed the time by swimming, shopping and watching the Welsh derby at Chepstow racecourse.

Amy and Jim had to wait nearly three weeks before the Atlantic weather turned in their favour. The Seafarer which had been especially adapted to carry the extra fuel needed for the journey finally left Pendine at midday on Saturday, July 22 1933.

Hostelry histories

Walk down any street in the centre of most South Wales towns and without realising it you will probably be walking back through history. There may well be fewer pubs around these days but those that remain continue to tell a tale often linked to the history of the area. Pub names were often inspired by religion, royalty, heroes and the occasional scandal. Knowing how to read the signs means being able to trace the history of the hostelry and learn much about its former customers.

A policeman on traffic point duty in a tram-lined High Street, Newport, early 1920s.

NEWPORT street snapshots

Charles Street, Newport, early 1900s.

IT'S SNOW

The winter of 1963 brought South Wales to its knees

During 1963 in South Wales 20ft high snowdrifts blocked roads and pavements. Lakes and rivers froze and huge blocks of ice were seen on a number of beaches.

Temperatures plummeted to minus 20 degrees which made the winter of 1962-3 the coldest since 1740 and the most severe of the 20th Century.

Some would contend that the winter of 1947 was even worse. It is difficult to compare the two, for how do you measure the scale of the ferocious weather that gripped South Wales in both winters? Suffice it to say that statistics record 1947 as having more snow and 1963 being colder with both causing abject misery for people whose daily lives suffered in every way.

Snow also brought serious problems in 1982 and a number of other subsequent years, but the white-out of 1963 will remain in the memory more than most for many people who experienced it.

South Wales was one of the UK areas hardest hit by the appalling conditions which began at the end of December 1962 when blizzards driven on by gale-force westerly winds resulted in 20ft deep snowdrifts. On New Year's Eve the snow turned to ice and roads and pavements became lethal skating rinks.

A group of playful Swansea schoolgirls prepare for a snowball fight in 1956.

An ambulance sent to rescue a farmer's wife who was seriously ill with peritonitis in the Vale of Glamorgan could only get to St Bride's Major a couple of miles away and her rescuers, four policemen and a civilian, had to battle through snowdrifts to reach her. Other villages in the Vale were also cut off and farmers could not reach livestock which starved to death.

Walking was often the only way of getting about that winter and even then it was a major struggle. Among those with tales to tell was Elwyn Davies who had to walk six miles through atrocious conditions to get to his job at Aberthaw power station because it was essential to keep it going during the big freeze. It was just as important to keep coal production underway, but with roads and pavements like sheets of glass miners were finding it difficult to get to their valley pits. Elsewhere factories closed because people could not get to work. Power lines were brought down and retired phone linesman, Val Pope of North Gower, had to struggle through mountainous snowdrifts in the upper Swansea Valley to restore vital communication links. The snow was higher than his van, he recalled.

In Newport two nurses had to walk miles to get to their hospital which was struggling to cope with the number of people with broken or fractured limbs after falling in the snow. Some of the town's tradesmen used sledges to deliver goods to customers while one man skied to work at Alcan Aluminium in Rogerstone.

January was probably the toughest month with mean monthly temperatures in South Wales more than five degrees centigrade below normal, although there was

JOKE!

A Ford Anglia car and its driver receive a helping hand as they struggle to climb a slippery Swansea hill in the depths of the winter of 1963.

The coldest winter for more than 200 years began with blizzards sweeping in on gale-force winds in December and didn't end until the early spring, recalls JONATHAN ISAACS.

little improvement in February. Icy roads caused 141 road accidents in the old county of Monmouthshire that January, three times the figure for the same month the previous year.

Villages high up in the valleys were badly affected with Tredegar, Ebbw Vale, Blaenavon and Brynmawr cut off at times during the winter. Schools stayed open if they could – more children used to walk to lessons then and the Health and Safety issues of today did not exist – but even so at one time in January 196 primary and 18 secondary schools in the county of Monmouthshire alone were forced to close because of damaged heating systems, frozen water supplies or frozen outside toilets.

As many as 2,000 children were sent home from schools in the Rhondda on January 21 because of frozen pipes

A two-car Valley Lines Sprinter train struggles away from Radyr with a service to Treherbert during heavy snow on January 31, 1991.

which affected the eleven-plus exams. South Wales householders lived in constant fear of water pipes bursting in their homes when their cold water tanks froze. By January 24 water was being rationed because the weather was making it difficult to get supplies from reservoirs. Carmarthen was one town to be hit by these emergency measures.

Life did go on, food reached the shops which was fine provided you could get to them. But there were fears of shortages, particularly of milk.

As January made way for February, then March arrived, it seemed as if the misery would never end. But suddenly, on the morning of March 6, South Wales people awoke to no frost for the first time since Boxing Day the previous year.

Rising temperatures arrived to release the area from its icy grip. The horrendous weather of that winter was caused by anticyclones to the north and east of the UK which brought bitterly cold air over the country, hitting South Wales particularly badly. What is so unusual is that it stayed for so long.

Will it ever get as bad again? According to the Met Office a winter like that of 1962-3 is expected to occur only once every 1,000 years or more.

It's a FACT

A disastrous fire gutted the interior of Margam Castle in Port Talbot in August 1977. The roof was brought down and the flames damaged chimneys and turrets as well as original gothic-style wall panelling.

Passengers would have had a long wait for any of these buses. They were marooned in Bridgend's normally busy bus station after heavy snow during the 1980s.

Thousands of vehicles daily normally use this road at Cimla, Neath. The snow of 1982 meant it was traffic free — for a day at least.

This is how they built their snowmen in the Afan Valley during the heavy fall of 1982!

For these youngsters at least heavy snow brought with it the chance to have some good clean fun.

Heroic act

Pilot died battling to save village

When test pilot James Wallace turned up for duty at RAF St Athan one cold January Monday in 1958 little did he realise that he was about to embark on what would be his last flight.

And though they would never have realised, as the minutes ticked by on the mantel clocks above the fireplaces keeping them warm in their neat and tidy terraced homes the residents of a West Wales village were in growing danger. Only the brave actions of the unassuming flyer would save many of their lives.

Flight Lieutenant Wallace's job that day was to put a Canberra WE117 jet aircraft through its paces on a routine air test. It was the kind of task he had safely and successfully accomplished many times both with this and other aircraft in his important role with 38 MU at St Athan in the Vale of Glamorgan.

On this occasion however things were destined to turn out differently and at a quarter to three that overcast afternoon, just 15 minutes into the flight, the Canberra seemed to suffer problems.

It was spotted by an eyewitness, flying in a westerly direction at around 500ft over Garngoch Common on the outskirts of Swansea. As they followed the course of the aircraft they suddenly heard the engine cut out, saw it dive to the right and vanish from their sight.

Meanwhile villagers at Llangennech, completely unaware of the danger heading their way carried on with their daily tasks. For some that meant getting ready to collect their children from the village school.

Just minutes later the peace of their tranquil village was shattered by a huge explosion. The doomed jet aircraft with James Wallace at the controls had fallen to earth. On hitting the ground the Canberra had exploded, rocking the foundations of many buildings in Llangennech village and forming a crater more than 30ft deep. Debris from the crash had been scattered for hundreds of yards in every direction.

The doomed plane had crashed onto marshland near Llangennech Railway Station on the Carmarthenshire-side of the Loughor Estuary.

Witnesses described how, during the last few seconds of its flight, the Canberra veered off its collision-course with Llangennech village before crashing into the marsh. There was no doubt that the change of direction had been instigated, at great cost, by the brave 35 year-old pilot. His unselfish action had without a shred of doubt saved many lives.

Would-be rescuers rushed to the scene to render assistance, but by the time they reached the edge of the crater the main wreckage was already beginning to sink and disappear under the surface. The only recognisable parts of the ill-fated aircraft which lay above ground was a pair of undercarriage wheels.

In the cold and fading mid-winter dusk a wider search of the marsh was made for the pilot, but his body was not located until the following day.

Any sign of the main impact point has long since disappeared due to the changing nature of tidal mudflats and the creation of drainage channels in the area. Small pieces of corroded aluminium can still be found around the crash site however.

Flight Lieutenant Wallace was born in South Shields, Tyne and Wear. Along with his academic achievements while at High School he became a champion swimmer winning many medals and on his death the Wallace family initiated and funded an annual school swimming trophy in his honour.

On leaving school he had followed in his father's footsteps and became a draughtsman at the Swan-

in the sky

James Wallace as a test pilot and alongside, in his early RAF days as a sergeant pilot during the Second World War.

Hunter ship-building yard, but in July 1941 he had enlisted as a pilot in the RAF. On completion of his training in Southern Rhodesia he served with 103 Squadron, Bomber Command. At the end of hostilities he married and returned to his pre-war occupation as a draughtsman. It seems it wasn't long before his passion for flying prompted him to re-enlist in the RAF, this time as a test pilot. Serving first at Linton-on-Ouse, he and his young family moved to St.Athan in 1952 where they stayed until the time of his accident. His daughter Jane recalled many trips with her father carrying out 'circuits and bumps' over the airfield in the station's Auster aircraft. He also participated in the Battle of Britain Open Days at St.Athan, thrilling the crowds at the well-attended event.

In November 1957, just two months before the crash at Llangennech, his services to the RAF were recognised when he was awarded the Air Force Cross at Buckingham Palace. James's flight on the fateful day of the accident was to be one of his last as a test-pilot, for he was shortly due to transfer to the RAF's prestigious Queen's Flight.

He was buried at Llantwit Cemetery, Boverton, a short distance away from the busy RAF base of St Athan here his ill-fated flight began.

— STEPHEN H JONES

LLANGENNECH PARISH COUNCIL

D. Gerald Roderick, Clerk.

40 Maes Road,
Llangennech,
Llanelly.

23rd January, 1958.

Mrs. G. E. Wallace,
14, Llantwit Road,
St. Athan,
Nr. Barry.

Dear Mrs. Wallace,

I understand from the Officer Commanding R.A.F. St. Athan that he has passed on to you my Council's deepest sympathies on the tragic death of your husband.

We, the villagers of Llangennech, are convinced that he sacrificed his own life in saving the lives of others, and I sincerely trust that perhaps this thought will help to strengthen and comfort you, in this sad period of your life.

Yours sincerely,

D. G. Roderick.

A letter of condolence sent by Llangennech Parish Council to the Wallace family soon after the accident.

IN AT THE DEEP END!

Many South Wales towns had the answer to keeping you cool on sunny summer days — an outdoor pool. JONATHAN ISAACS recalls some of them, but many more will be remembered with affection.

WHEN they were built in the late 1920s and early 1930s outdoor swimming pools were considered luxurious, a great asset for the South Wales valleys where there few facilities for the children at the time.

Such pools, or lidos as they were often referred to, were new and exciting, a place for fun as well as being somewhere where you could learn to swim.

As a small boy living in the Rhondda Valley, I remember my grandfather still extolling their virtues more than 30 years later.

"You're lucky, that's where we had to go," he said, pointing to the local river. Pits were still working in the valley at the time and the River Rhondda was as black as pitch. If you had the courage to put your hand into the icy water it disappeared and I could only wonder at the remarkable toughness of the valley men who grew up in such hard times 100 years ago.

An alternative to the river, and somewhat cleaner, was somewhere we called 'the feeder', a dam behind a high wall on the mountainside above Tonypandy which once served the pit below. It was used by generations of local boys and was incredibly dangerous, being very

Swimmers gather round the diving board at the Lido, Bedwellty Park, Tredegar, late 1920s and inset, the pool's pavilion.

deep and breathtakingly cold, but to plunge into the water on a hot summer's day was wonderfully refreshing. This was no place for modesty and you swam naked but luckily it was pretty isolated and anyone passing was likely to be male.

The outdoor swimming pools were just as cold but looked more enticing and at least had reasonable facilities. The 30 or so that were built in the valleys around 80 years ago were basically the same.

You entered through turnstiles and changed in wooden huts surrounding the pool, the male and female facilities on opposite sides. Woe betide anyone caught on the wrong side! The pool's base was painted a bright, sky blue which on sunny days made the water sparkle and appear incredibly inviting — until you jumped in. The cold was a shock to the senses and it was a hardy soul indeed who managed to stay in for more than a few minutes.

SPLISH, SPLOSH, SPLASH!

There were two pools near my Tonypandy home, one was in Porth and the other in Gelligaled Park in Ystrad, the first public lido in the Rhondda which opened in 1934. For some reason we always went to Gelligaled, perhaps because this was where our school went for swimming lessons.

Every Wednesday morning from the end of May until the start of the school summer holidays our teacher would take around 30 of us two miles on the bus to Gelligaled and the miracle was that we learned to swim at all given the short time we managed to stay in the water. I remember the teacher looking out of the school window one cloudy, windy Wednesday.

"I'll take you swimming today but I don't think you'll be in for more than a few minutes," he said. He was optimistic. We jumped in, everyone shrieked as the cold hit us, and we immediately jumped out again and refused to go back.

Our cold summers were obviously a major problem for outdoor lidos.They cost a lot of money to run but were only open for around three months of the year. Even then, they were only busy on warm, sunny days.

Remarkably, despite these disadvantages, a few South Wales outdoor pools managed to remain open until quite recently. One of these was The Knap lido in Barry which was one of the largest open air pools in the UK. It was 120 yards long and 30 yards wide and held more than a million gallons of water.

At one time it had a water polo team, a swimming club and a lifeguard club. Thousands of people went to see the Welsh Swimming Championships held there in July 1937. Built in the 1920s by people unable to find work at the time, The Knap's heyday was in the 1950s when 3,000 people visited the pool at weekends and 1,500 every day during the summer school holidays.

But the cost of running the pool was enormous and it was neglected and abandoned in the 1990s before the site was redeveloped in 2004.

A similar fate befell Hendy swimming pool near Pontarddulais, despite a long campaign by local people to try and save it. As with other outdoor lidos in South Wales, it was a much loved facility where generations of youngsters had learned to swim. Built by miners who worked on it voluntarily, it opened in 1933 but was forced to close in 2002 because of health concerns. It needed £500,000 in repairs and running costs had to be added to this figure so the fight to re-open it was reluctantly abandoned in 2008 and the pool was demolished in 2009.

There are still hopes that Brynamman pool in the Amman Valley can be saved, although it has not opened since 2009. It was the last outdoor lido in South Wales until its closure caused by the cost of repairs, which was put at £300,000. The pool, which received 2,000 visits each summer, still has most of its original features, including the turnstiles and wooden changing huts. It was built more than 80 years ago, again by the unemployed who had the choice for wages of a packet of 10 Woodbine cigarettes a day or a bar of chocolate.

Most of the other South Wales outdoor pools have long since been demolished and their sites redeveloped. Gelligaled was filled in when Rhondda Leisure Centre and its plush indoor heated pool was built in the early 1980s. But remarkably, a

The once popular pools at Ynysangharad Park, Pontypridd.

much better fate awaits another valley outdoor pool that closed more than 20 years ago.

Thanks to the Heritage Lottery Fund, Pontypridd lido in the town's Ynysangharad Memorial Park is being refurbished as part of a £6.2 million project. Built in 1927 and closed in 1991, the listed lido was used by the town's most famous son, singer Tom Jones, and Jenny James from Treforest, the first woman to swim the English Channel in 1951, trained there. It is planned to have it open by spring 2014 and hopefully 30,000 people a year will swim there.

What makes its developers so optimistic? Unlike the outdoor lidos of the past, the new pool will be heated.

There are almost more bodies than water in this busy sunny summer day snapshot of Victoria Park paddling pool, Cardiff in the 1950s. It's not surprising perhaps that it was so popular. It was and still is the capital city's only municipal paddling pool. Cardiff historian BRIAN LEE recalls the tale of Billy the seal, one of the pool's most famous swimmers. Accidentally caught by fishermen in the Irish Sea, he was discovered in a box of fish bought by a Cardiff market stallholder. He was presented to the council who gave him a home in the pool. Unsurprisingly he became a star attraction there during the 1930s.

The popular Lido at Bedwellty Park was 200ft long and 50ft wide.

Paradise

Clydach pool was the first

Clydach swimming pool, above, was completed and opened in 1935. The then Rhyndwyclydach Parish Council was the first parish council in Great Britain to build an open air pool.

The pool was 10 yards wide and 33 yards long. The water depth at the shallow end was 2 ft 8 ins, and at the deep end 9 ft. Alongside the main pool there was a small pool for babies to learn to swim. There was also a five stage diving stand and a springboard at the deep end.

Water to fill the pool was drawn from the Lower Clydach river. The water passed through a filtration tank and once the pool was full the process was changed and the water pumped from the deep end back through the filter tank into the shallow end. The filter tank contained a special grade of sand and gravel. The water after leaving the tank, passed through a cascade aerator and before re-entering the pool liquid chlorine, light sodium carbonate and aluminium sulphate was added to it. When the tank needed cleaning, the flow was reversed and all the dirt washed into a sewer.

Scorching hot summer days often meant one thing when we were kids — Clydach open-air baths. My three boy cousins and I would jump on a bus in Pontardawe and set off on the short journey down the Swansea Valley.

We wouldn't be alone. There would be others like us making the same pilgrimage to the watery magnet.

It wasn't hard to work out who else on the bus was actually heading there. They all carried a hastily grabbed towel rolled up under their arms!

The journey ended with everyone piling off the bus in the middle of Clydach and joining a mad stampede to be first to reach the pool.

The obstacle course to get there involved dashing up a flight of stone steps, handing over your pennies to get in, trotting across the slippery poolside before reaching the changing rooms. Rooms is a grand way of describing what was just a row of little cubicles. They seemed a bit run down, were about three feet by four feet and though it never seemed to bother my cousins, this shy little girl was mortified by the foot or more gap at the bottom of the door. Worse still the doors never locked properly and you always ran the risk of someone pushing in.

I quickly learned that wearing my frilly skirted, blue bather under my clothes gave me some reassurance and also had a great impact on the speed with which I got undressed and then afterwards dried myself and got dressed again.

at the poolside

Sunny day smiles at South Wales swim pools.

Fascinating memories of the way many people kept their cool on distant summer days in the Swansea Valley are recalled by CHERYL ROBERTS.

Despite all that I couldn't wait to get into the crowded pool, even though I couldn't swim. The shallow end was my usual spot, though even shy little girls can be daring and sometimes I would gingerly edge my way towards the point where the pool floor began sloping into the deep end.

I'll never forget getting into the pool. The weather might have been hot and the pool may have looked inviting, but the water was so cold it initially took my breath away.

My cousins weren't the slightest bit bothered about that and raced from the changing rooms to the poolside before launching themselves in without a thought. Before long they would be climbing onto the diving board and showing off by plummeting into the water and splashing everyone around them.

Looking back, it was a simple pleasure, but the stuff that unforgettable memories of glorious summers when the sun seemed to shine endlessly.

Happy days!

The movie made

RICHARD Burton, Anthony Hopkins, Catherine Zeta Jones . . . these are the star names most likely to come to mind when anyone thinks of actors from South Wales who have made it big in Hollywood.

But there have been many more who have made that trip across the Atlantic on a quest for fame and fortune, some of them successfully, others less so.

In fact, the links between South Wales and Hollywood stretch back nearly 100 years, to the days of silent films when looks and gestures were more important than the spoken word. One of the first South Wales-born actors to wow America was Gareth Hughes, born in Llanelli in 1894. Gareth Hughes seems a most unlikely name for a Hollywood star, today it would probably be changed for something like Gary Hugo, but he actually chose it as his stage name. He was named by his working class family as William John Hughes and was a chemist's apprentice who did some local amateur acting before walking to London at the age of 15 to seek his glory.

There he joined a West End theatre-based group of players which went on a tour of the United States. Gareth was talent spotted in New York and left the group to take a series of minor roles on Broadway. He was persuaded to take his chances in the up and coming silent movies business where he was usually cast as a young and callow, sensitive hero.

Gruffydd

Michael Sheen

hearthrobs in Wales

Gareth made as many as 45 films between 1918 and 1931 and even took top billing over Rudolph Valentino in the 1919 film Eyes of Youth, but it was Sentimental Tommy in 1921 that made him a star with Paramount Pictures. At the height of his fame he was earning 2,000 dollars a week, the equivalent of £26,000 today.

But misfortune came with the Wall Street crash of 1929 and he was left penniless. Although he continued making films for another two years his star was fading fast. Talking pictures had arrived and his Llanelli accent did not go down well with cinema audiences. Gareth returned to South Wales in 1958 intending to spend his remaining years in the town of his birth. But he missed the sun and after just five months he returned to California where he died on October 1,1965. A plaque to his memory was unveiled in 2010 at his former home in Princess Street, Llanelli.

Richard Burton

Ivor Novello was described by those who knew him as a 'truly beautiful man.' But this was no Italian heart-throb. He was born David Ivor Davies in Cardiff in 1893, the son of a council rent collector, and his stage name came from his middle name and the maiden name of his mother. Ivor was a composer, singer and actor who became one of the most popular British entertainers of

It's a FACT

Port Talbot-born actor Sir Anthony Hopkins made his first professional appearance at the Palace Theatre, Swansea, in 1960 with Swansea Little Theatre's production of Have a Cigarette.

Starring

Sian Phillips

Gareth Hughes

Rachel Roberts

Rhys Ifans

the first half of the 20th Century. His first big hit was 'Keep the Home Fires Burning' which was tremendously popular during the First World War and brought Novello money and fame at the age of just 21.

He turned to acting in the 1920s and went to Hollywood where he made his movie debut in 1923 in The White Rose. But his career in Tinsel Town was not a success. Although he accepted a contract to write for and appear in films for MGM, his main work was writing the dialogue for Tarzan the Ape Man. 'Me Tarzan-you Jane' was way beneath his talents and disillusioned he returned to London where his musicals dominated the theatre from the mid-1930s to the early 1950s.

Ray Milland was one of Hollywood's most bankable and durable stars from 1934 to 1948. He was born in Neath in 1907 and named Alfred Reginald Jones, son of Elizabeth Annie and Alfred Jones. He may have taken his stage name from the town's Millands area, although there are several versions of the story.

There was little in his youth to indicate he would become an actor and at the age of 21 he went to London as a member of the elite Household Cavalry. In 1929 he befriended actress Estelle Brody who introduced him to a producer friend. They persuaded Ray to appear in a motion picture bit part and the following year he was signed by MGM and went to Hollywood, although his big break did not come until 1934 when he joined Paramount where he stayed for most of his career which continued until 1985.

His best films are reckoned to be his Academy Award-winning portrayal of an alcoholic writer in The Lost Weekend in 1945 opposite John Wayne in the 1942 film Reap the Wild Wind; and as a husband plotting murder in Dial M for Murder in 1954 when an off-screen affair with his co-star, Grace Kelly, is said to have almost wrecked both their careers. During the latter part of his career he appeared in many forgettable films and when asked why replied: "For the money, old chap, for the money."

He added: "My philosophy is do what you can with what you've got. I know actors from my generation who cry, 'why don't they send me any scripts?' I tell them, 'because you still think of yourself as a leading man. You're 68, not 38. Face it'."

Ray Milland died of lung cancer in Torrance, California, on March 10, 1986. He was aged 79.

Fiery Llanelli-born actress Rachel Roberts' best work was British, but she appeared in supporting roles in several American films after relocating to Hollywood in the early 1970s. Her roles included Foul Play in 1978 and as Mrs Dangers in her last film, Charlie Chan and the Curse of the Dragon Queen released a year after her death.

Born in September 1927, she rebelled against her Baptist upbringing. Her career began at a Swansea repertory company in 1950 and took off in 1960 with her portrayal of Brenda in Karel Reisz's Saturday Night and Sunday Morning which won her a British Academy Film Award.

She married the love of her life, the actor Rex Harrison, in 1962 and was devastated when they divorced 11 years later. The strain of the affair showed in an interview in which she said: "It is very difficult to be taken seriously when you're introduced as the fourth Mrs Rex Harrison."

Stanley Baker

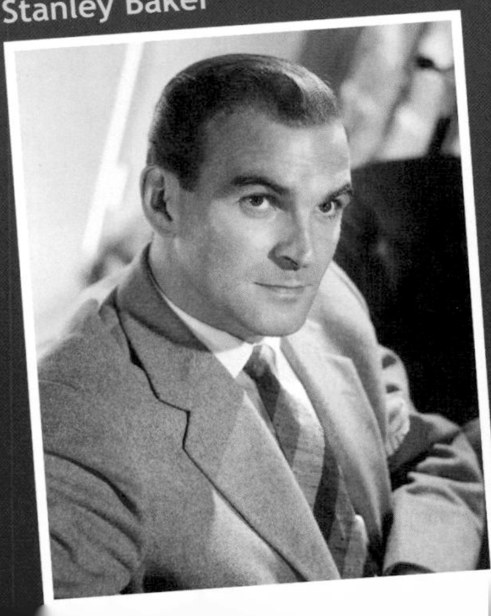

roles

John Rhys-Davies

Even so she tried to win him back but it was futile and she committed suicide by taking an overdose of barbiturates and alcohol on November 26, 1980, at her home in Los Angeles. She was 53.

The Rhondda's Stanley Baker was just 48 when he died in 1976 but crammed enough zest and energy in his short life to fill three or four lifetimes.

He was a contemporary and drinking buddy of Richard Burton who introduced him to the actress Ellen Martin. They married in 1950.

With his rugged good looks and impeccable delivery, Stanley Baker, who became Sir Stanley just weeks before his death, was one of the most highly-regarded and sought after stars of his generation. His list of film credits goes back to 1943 but it was as Lieutenant John Chard VC in the 1964 epic, Zulu, for which he is best known. Shortly before he died he was planning to produce a sequel, Zulu Dawn.

The role which shot him to fame was as the cowardly Bennett in the 1953 film, The Cruel Sea. Offers followed from Hollywood beginning with the part of Sir Mordred in The Knights of the Round Table, also in 1953. His output was prodigious, he made at least one film most years throughout his career, sometimes as many as three or four, and there were television parts and stage roles as well.

Amazingly he found time to engage in business activities. He formed his own production company, Diamond Films, followed by Oakhurst Productions, and helped set up Great Western Enterprises which was involved in entertainment projects, notably music concerts. Sir Stanley was also one of the founder members of Harlech Television and continued to be a director until his death.

"The acting bit is great for the ego, all the real excitement is in business," he said. "I'm still surprised how good I am at business."

But the British film industry was in decline in the late 1960s and many of the Oakhurst films failed at the Box Office. When the Stock Market crashed in 1973 Sir Stanley's enterprises were in deep trouble and he was forced to accept roles in truly abysmal films to keep afloat. Things were made worse by his compulsive gambling, although he always insisted he had enough money to care for his family.

His health was also deteriorating, he had always been a

diagnosed with lung cancer. Surgery was not successful and he died in June that year in Malaga, Spain.

His ashes were scattered over Llanwonno mountain, above Ferndale, the valley village where he was born in February 1928. Other actors who have had roles in Hollywood include Sian Phillips, from Gwaun-cae-Gurwen in the Amman Valley. Although it is as the scheming poisoner Livia in the television series I Claudius (1976) that she is probably best known, she has had an immensely varied career, ranging from a newsreader with BBC Wales to top stage and film parts.

Born just a few miles from Sian in Ammanford, but in 1944, is John Rhys-Davies, who also appeared in I Claudius as Makro, leader of the Praetorian guard under the mad emperor, Caligula. Roles for which he is best known include the charismatic Arab excavator, Sallah, in the Indiana Jones films; General Leonid Pushkin from the James Bond film, The Living Daylights; and as Gimli the dwarf in the The Lord of the Rings trilogy.

The list of South Wales stars to have gone to Hollywood is growing all the time and this looks likely to continue. The stature of Michael Sheen, brought up in Port Talbot, is ever rising and Ioan Gruffudd of Cardiff has became a well respected and sought after star after his early role in Titanic. Others to have made their mark include Matthew Rhys of Cardiff and Rhys Ifans, born in Haverfordwest.

With home grown talents like these, South Wales is set to stay firmly on the Hollywood map. Here's to

Y Ddraig Goch

The Red Dragon

Simply RED

Take your pick! From roses to lipstick, red seems to have been the hottest colour in the palette since the beginning of time.

But wait a minute. Have you ever stopped to think about how it plays a much more important part in our everyday lives.

From the red dragon that proudly adorns our national flag to the rugby strip that almost every young boy in the Principality would be proud to wear and win in, the colour red seems to tell a significant tale.

One of the brightest in the artist's palette, it seems to ooze importance and quality. It certainly steals attention wherever it appears.

Just look at some of the images on this page of everyday street furniture and everyday vehicles from down the years to discover the proof! From buses to lorries, fire service vehicles to Post Office pillar boxes, it's hard to escape the effect the hue has had on our daily lives. In fact red is supposedly the first colour ever perceived by man. The pictures on these pages tell just some of the fascinating, brightly coloured story!

When it comes to colour in our everyday lives there is one hue in the painter's pot that seems to have played its part more than most down the years – RED!

Buses

Lorries

Kiosks

Fire engines

Vans

Dictionary definition:

RED

/re d/, [rĕd]
noun, adjective, red·der, red·dest.
Any of various colours resembling the colour of blood; the primary colour at one extreme end of the visible spectrum.

A busy day at Bridgend bus station, 1962.

Bygone Bridgend

Like many towns across South Wales, Bridgend can trace its origins back to the earliest times. The pictures here offer a hint of how the town evolved down many decades.

A 1920s snapshot of life in the centre of Bridgend.

J.B.RICHAR
FAMILY BUTC

A train passes through Bridgend station, with the town centre in the background, 1974.

Nolton Street had lots of shops, but little traffic it seems, in the days when the photographer captured the attention of everyone.

JONATHAN ISAACS remembers ring-side times

When the valleys packed a real

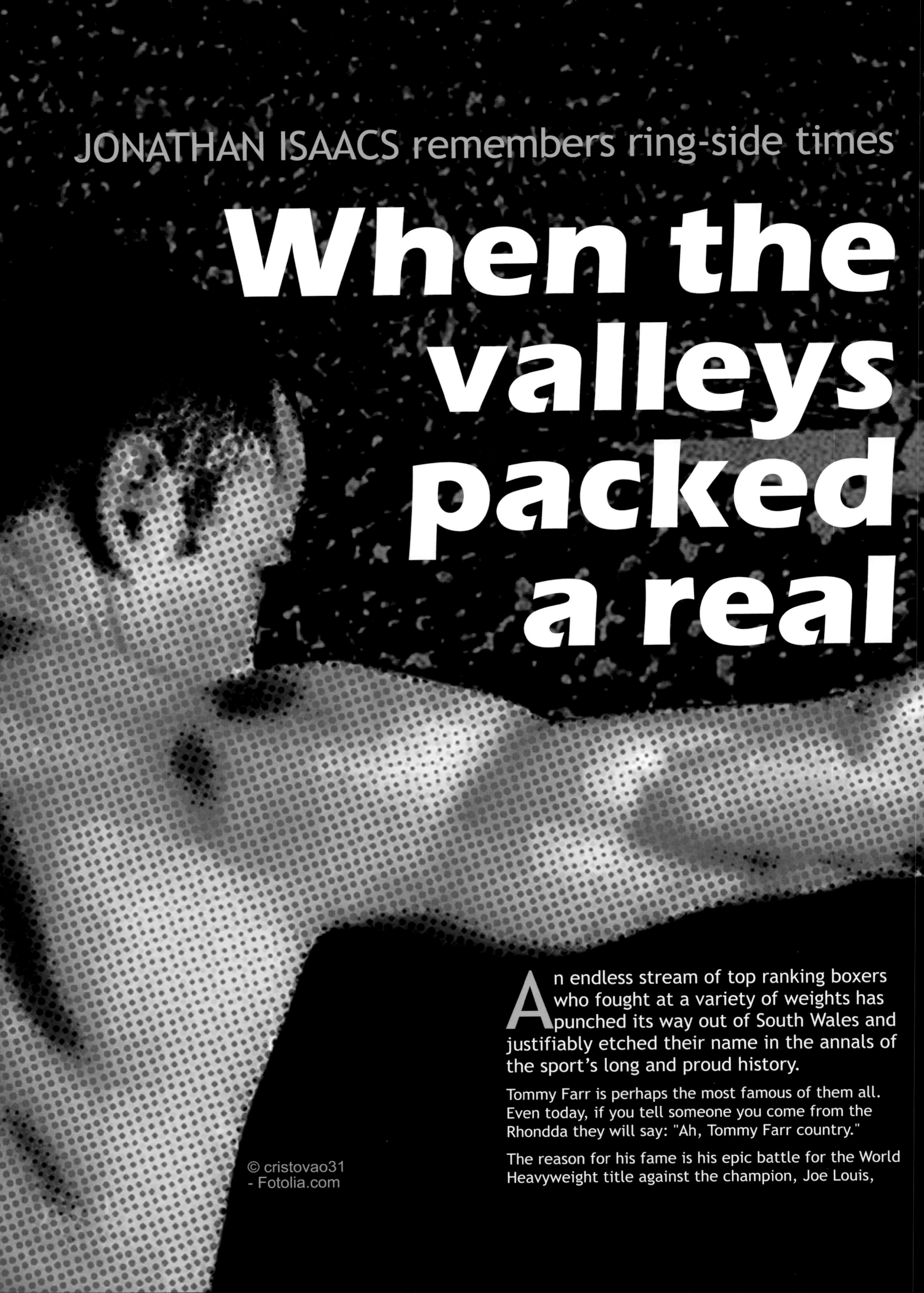

© cristovao31 - Fotolia.com

An endless stream of top ranking boxers who fought at a variety of weights has punched its way out of South Wales and justifiably etched their name in the annals of the sport's long and proud history.

Tommy Farr is perhaps the most famous of them all. Even today, if you tell someone you come from the Rhondda they will say: "Ah, Tommy Farr country."

The reason for his fame is his epic battle for the World Heavyweight title against the champion, Joe Louis,

before a crowd of 32,000 in New York in August 1937. It was Louis' first defence of the title and no-one gave Tommy any hope of winning. Louis himself saw it only as a warm-up match before he met stronger opponents. Tommy however, nicknamed The Tonypandy Terror, was not going to play it the American's way.

Louis was a strong, powerful and fearsome boxer and Tommy was just 23. But he had been fighting since the age of 12 and had earned a reputation the hard way, through the boxing booths that were common in the South Wales valleys at the time.

Tommy was born into poverty in Clydach Vale, near Tonypandy in the Rhondda Valley, in March 1914. Like the other boys of his time, the mine offered the only employment and Tommy hated it. Boxing was his way out. He wasn't even a teenager when he fought for the first time in the infamous local boxing booths and by the time he met Louis that never to be forgotten night in New York's Yankee Stadium, just over a decade later he had more than 200 fights under his belt.

Everyone in the valleys was glued to their radio that night and even though Tommy was British and Empire heavyweight champion he was considered to be no match for Louis. But 'The Terror' was to prove them wrong. He fearlessly attacked and defended against the more experienced 'Brown Bomber' and took him the full 15 rounds. It was a ferocious battle: "My face looked like a dug up road," Tommy said afterwards.

PROGRAMME

GREAT HEAVY-WEIGHT CONTEST—12 3-MINUTE ROUNDS.

JIMMY WILDE

SWANSEA

(Heavy-weight Champion of Wales)

V.

SALAH EL DIN

(Heavy-weight Champion of Egypt)

SENSATIONAL RETURN CONTEST—10 3-MINUTE ROUNDS.

BOYO REES

ABERCWMBOI

(Light-weight Champion of Wales)

V

TOMMY JOHN

(LONDON)

Lords

He lost on points but won worldwide respect. After the Louis fight, Tommy cashed in on his fame and fought unsuccessful bouts at Madison Square Garden in New York. By 1940 boxing had made the boy from the valleys a rich man and he was able to retire. But he suffered major financial problems and was facing bankruptcy when he decided to make a comeback 10 years' later.

But by now he was 36 and although he regained the Wales Heavyweight title he lost to Don Cockell in seven rounds in Birmingham three years later. In typical Tommy fashion, he sang the Welsh National Anthem at the ringside, then announced his retirement. He was three days short of his 39th birthday.

In his professional career, Tommy had won 81 of his 126 professional fights, 24 of them by knockout. He died in March 1986 at the age of 72.

The Tylorstown Terror

JIMMY WILDE is regarded by many as the greatest ever flyweight boxer. Some will go even further and contend that he is the greatest boxer of all time.

But this son of a coal miner, born in Quakers Yard near Merthyr Tydfil in May 1892, was tiny and frail looking. He was only around 5ft tall and his weight never reached eight stone. When he worked down the pit he was sent to crawl through spaces none of the other pitmen could get through.

But he was tough, very tough, as his nicknames testify: The Mighty Atom, The Tylorstown Terror and The Ghost with a Hammer in his Hand. Jimmy, whose family later moved to Tylorstown in the Rhondda, had ferocious strength that enabled him to beat opponents who were much larger and heavier.

He built up his strength in the mines and at the boxing booths that were popular in the early years of the last century. Jimmy, like other fighters, would stand on a stage at shows and fairs as they toured the mining villages and promoters would encourage the local men to take them on. Anyone could try

of the ring

The bronze statue commemorating the achievements of Howard Winstone, which can be seen at the Beacons Centre, Merthyr.

their hand and Jimmy had been known to beat as many as 22 opponents in one day, although it has to be said they were often drunks who had just stumbled out of the local pub or club. But there was money to be had, as much as £3 a day if the fighter was particularly good, much better than the wages down the pit. Jimmy fought hundreds of boxing booth bouts, winning most of them. The statistics show he also won 130 of his 149 professional fights, losing only four and drawing 15, a hugely impressive record. He became the first officially recognised World Flyweight Champion on December 18, 1916, when he defeated Zulu Kid of America but took a hammering when he defended his title against Pancho Villa in New York in June 1923.

Pancho was just 22, Jimmy was 31 and he was so badly beaten that he temporarily lost his memory afterwards and did not recognise his wife Elizabeth for three weeks. Sensibly, he decided to retire.

For the last years of his life he lived in Barry and was involved in several business interests, including a cinema chain. He was also a partner in a cafe in Barry Island, called, appropriately enough, The Mighty Atom. But the ventures failed and he ended his life as it had begun, in poverty.

The brave Jimmy Wilde was mugged at a railway station in 1965 and never properly recovered. He died at a Cardiff hospital in 1969.

The Welsh Wizard

HOWARD WINSTONE was a magical boxer, hence his nickname, The Welsh Wizard. He won 61 of his 67 professional fights and lost only six even though he had lost the tips of three fingers of his right hand in an accident at the toy factory where he worked in his home town, Merthyr Tydfil.

It meant he had to adapt his boxing style but his courage and determination enabled him to overcome the problem. As an amateur he won the Amateur Boxing Association's bantamweight title in 1958 and the same year got the bantamweight gold medal at the Commonwealth Games in Cardiff, the only Welsh gold medal won at the games. He turned professional as a featherweight in 1959 and won all 34 of his first contests. Howard picked up the European title and defended it successfully seven times but

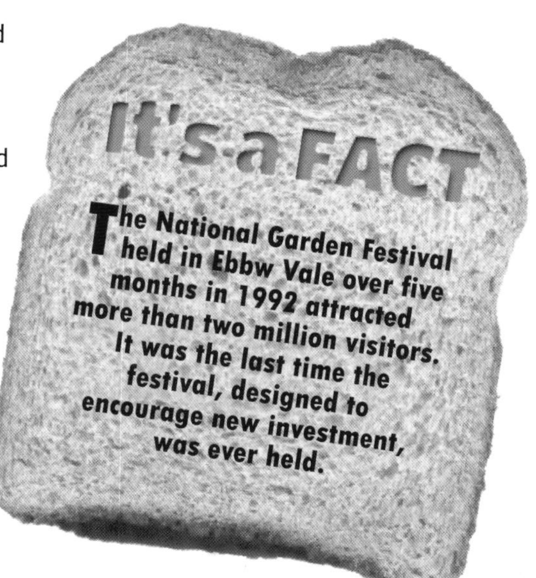

The other South Wales Warriors

IT is hard to know where to stop when tracking down some of the boxers who have plied their trade from South Wales. Here are just some who hit the headlines in their heyday:

'Peerless' Jim Driscoll was born in poverty in Cardiff in December 1880 and to escape he began boxing in fairground booths. In 1901 he turned professional and took the British Featherweight title by defeating Jim Bowker in a 15-round contest at the National Sporting Club in London in 1906.Two years later Jim became Commonwealth Featherweight champion and was the first featherweight to win a coveted Lonsdale Belt in 1910. He always stayed close to his beloved Cardiff and when he died at the age of 44 in 1925 more than 100,000 lined the city's streets for his funeral.

Percy Jones from the Rhondda was the first Welshman to hold a world boxing title. He took the World Flyweight title from Bill Ladbury over 20 rounds in 1914. Born to a mining family from Porth on Boxing Day, 1892, he is regarded as one of Wales' greatest boxers who never gained the recognition he deserved.

David 'Bomber' Pearce was an undefeated British Heavyweight boxing champion whose life ended tragically early. Born in Newport in 1959, he was one of seven boxing brothers and won his title by beating the holder, Swansea's Neville Meade, in 1983. But David's career suffered a severe blow when he was beaten in a European title fight by Lucien Rodriguez in March 1984. He was diagnosed with a brain abnormality and the British Boxing Board of Control withdrew his licence and declared his title vacant.

Neville Meade was a big-hitting heavyweight who won the Welsh and British heavyweight titles. Born in Jamaica in September 1948, he moved to Swansea with his family when he was nine and discovered boxing. His professional record is 34 fights and 20 wins, 18 of them by knockout.

the world title appeared to elude him until his memorable encounter with Mitsunori Seki of Japan in nine rounds at London's Royal Albert Hall in January 1968.

Howard was now World Featherweight Champion but he was finding it difficult to keep his weight down to the nine stone featherweight limit.

He made the first defence of his title in July 1968 at Porthcawl against Jose Legra and it ended in failure. Howard was knocked down twice in the first round and was suffering a badly swollen left eye before the bout was stopped in five rounds. He had lost his title and announced his retirement from boxing at the age of 29.

But he ended his career as a hero in Merthyr, where he was born on April 15, 1939. A tremendously popular figure in the town, he was also respected across Wales and was voted BBC Wales Sports Personality of the Year three times, in 1958, 1963 and 1967. He also received the MBE. Howard died in September 2000 aged 61. A film of his life, Risen, was made in 2011.

Jones The Punch

COLIN JONES was a big hitter, he had a ferocious left hook and 23 of his 26 professional fight victories were knockouts.

A British, Commonwealth and European champion, Colin was born in March, 1959, at Gorseinon, Swansea, into a family that encouraged his love of boxing.

He was just nine when a boxing club opened near the family home and, as Colin says, he was there from day one. His punch power won him three British schoolboy crowns.

He was just 17 when he was chosen for the Great Britain boxing team at the Olympic Games in Montreal, Canada, in 1976, the youngest British boxer

Boxer Colin Jones, mobbed on his return to Swansea, after winning the Commonwealth and European Championship, in 1981.

to qualify at an Olympic Games before the slightly younger Amir Khan in 2004. Colin turned professional and that powerful punch was to stand him in good stead. He also had the advantage of the legendary Eddie Thomas of Merthyr as his manager. Win followed win and in 1980 Colin was ready to take on the British Welterweight champion, Kirkland Laing.

Now Colin was to show how much he deserved his nickname, The Punch. Laing was an incredibly gifted boxer but a very different one from Colin. He literally danced round the ring, displaying amazing reflexes and dazzling footwork. Colin was slower but had the more powerful punch. The question was, whose style would be victorious?

It took nine rounds to find out. Colin landed a killer right-handed punch to Laing's jaw-and the end followed swiftly. Colin came home to Gorseinon the new British Welterweight Champion.

The Commonwealth and European titles followed and after a bout of appendicitis that put Colin out of boxing for 10 months he was ready to try for a world title.

His opponent in 1982 for the WBC title vacated by Sugar Ray Leonard was Milton McCrory, aka The Iceman. Colin was the underdog but the bout went the full 12 rounds and the match ended in a draw. Pubs and clubs across South Wales were packed the night of the rematch which was held in Las Vegas.

Again the fight went the distance but this time McCrory took the title in a split decision. It made little difference to the people of Swansea who lined the streets to give Colin a hero's welcome home a few days later. He made another stab at a world title, this time the WBA crown in 1985, when he took on Don Curry. But Colin suffered a deep cut to the bridge of his nose and the fight was stopped in the fourth round. Colin retired from professional boxing shortly afterwards aged 26.

The Matchstick Man

JOHNNY OWEN was nicknamed The Matchstick Man but like the great Jimmy Wilde his looks belied tremendous strength. His life was tragically short and what he might have achieved in boxing can only be wondered at. But his few years in the ring have left a tremendous legacy and his sportsmanship, courage and tenacity will always be inspirational for the generations who follow.

One of eight children, Johnny was born in Merthyr Tydfil in 1956. He began boxing at the age of eight and could often be seen pounding up and down the steep, hilly streets around the town building up his strength for the ring.

He turned professional in 1976 and two years later battled with Paul Ferrari of Australia for the vacant Commonwealth Bantamweight title. The bout went the full 15 rounds and is regarded as one of Johnny's finest performances. He returned to Merthyr as Wales's first ever holder of Bantamweight Champion of the Commonwealth.

Now Johnny moved on for the European title but his clash with the champion, Juan Francisco Rodriguez of Spain, was hugely controversial. It is claimed the champion's side got up to all kinds of dirty tricks to see their man win, even down to denying Johnny much needed sleep.

Even so many believed the Merthyr boxer had done enough to win so the decision to give the fight to Rodriguez was hugely controversial. The bout, in Spain, was Johnny's first professional defeat but he avenged himself in the return match held in Ebbw Vale 12 months later.

Johnny's last fight was in Los Angeles on September 19,1980. At stake was the WBC World Bantamweight title and with 12 seconds of the 12th round to go his opponent, Lupe Pintor, came at him with a right punch that sent him sprawling on the canvas where he stayed for the count.

Johnny never regained consciousness. Despite emergency surgery he fell into a coma and died seven weeks later. He was just 24.

The statue of boxer Johnny Owen which can be seen at Merthyr Tydfil.

Corona was

From the 1920s through to the end of the 1980s the sight and sound of the Corona pop man meant delight for thousands of children across South Wales and beyond as PHIL CARRADICE recalls.

It was a Welsh success story that has gone down in legend and remains an important part of the country's social history. Corona drinks were for so many years, delivered to the doors of houses across the land, first by horse and cart and then by lorry. And it all began with a small factory in Porth at the foot of the Rhondda valleys.

First the pop came by horse and cart.

The pop — carbonated beverage to give it the correct name — was produced by the Corona Soft Drinks Company, a firm that had been created by two Rhondda grocers, William Evans and William Thomas. The original factory opened in the 1890s under the name of Welsh Hills Mineral Waters, the name Corona only being adopted in the 1920s as the company expanded its range of activities to include all of Wales and many parts of England.

Temperance movement

The firm had its origins in the Temperance movement that was so strong in Britain during the final years of the 19th century. The Rhondda Valleys at this time were in the grip of the 'coal rush.' They were full of coal mines and the pubs of the region did a thriving business as men, after a day down the pit, were desperate to quench their thirst. As a result drunkenness was rife.

Grocers Evans and Thomas from Porth were determined to find an alternative drink for the miners. They had already been introduced to soft drinks by a peddler from West Wales — artificial carbonated mineral water had been first produced by Joseph Schweppe in Switzerland in the 18th century and so it was not a new invention. The problem had always been how to keep the fizz in the bottle.To begin with manufacturers simply hammered in a cork and wired it tight - a solution that was only partially successful. But then American Hiram Codd invented a revolutionary new system. It involved fitting each bottle with a glass marble, a rubber washer and a swing top that forced the marble into the neck of the bottle, so forming a tight seal. The rest, as they say, is history.

After visiting several manufacturers of carbonated mineral waters - in order to see how it was done - Evans and Thomas were ready for business. Their Porth factory was equipped with state of the art machinery in order to bottle the liquids and to clean empty bottles. But although the factory soon became a local landmark, sale of the fizzy drinks had little effect on drunkenness. And so it was decided that the product should be sold, door to door. Over 200 salesmen, each driving a horse and

Corona lorries were, more often than not, painted in the brightest, most attractive colours.

top of the pops

cart, were soon operating across South Wales. They sold a wide range of drinks, starting with the original orangeade and then moving on to others such as limeade and cherryade. More exotic flavours such as American cream soda and dandelion and burdock were soon added to the list.

The fizzy drinks may not have stopped drunkenness but they were hugely popular with all sections of society. And they had an immediate appeal for children who were soon drinking large quantities of the product. Parents quickly learned that it was best to ration the distribution of the gassy liquid.

Money back on the bottle

The glass bottles in which the pop was sold were a valuable commodity and, from the beginning, the company operated a system of money back on the ottle', thus ensuring that generations of school children would augment their pocket money by collecting discarded bottles and turning them in to shops and door to door sellers.

The door to door deliveries proved so successful that further factories were opened in places such as Pengam, Maesteg and Bridgend. By 1934 the Porth depot alone was operating 74 motor vehicles — three years later there were over 200 vehicles.

The outbreak of World War Two caused the company some disruption with lorries - and drivers - being commandeered for war service but soon after 1945 things were back to normal and the Corona pop man was back on his rounds.

William Evans, the guiding force behind the company, died in 1934 but the company continued to expand with his brother Frank assuming control. By the end of the 1930s over 170 million bottles of Corona pop were being produced each year - and most of it was sold by the delivery man who came each week to people's doors.

The Pop Factory

The Corona company was bought out by the Beecham Group in 1958 and was transferred to Britvic in 1987. The Porth plant closed the same year and the old factory was converted into a music and recording studio. The link with Corona was maintained when, in 2000, the studio was christened The Pop Factory. The fizzy drink continued to sell, and its advertising slogan 'Every bubble's passed its FIZZICAL' was seen on television and chanted by children for many more years.

With the advent of supermarkets, however, the need for door to door delivery gradually dropped away. By the end of the 1980s they were a luxury and like the milk, bread and fish vans that had plied their trade around the streets for years, the Corona delivery man was soon a thing of the past. It didn't stop the sale of the product, it just meant that the personal door to door touch had gone.

The Corona pop man remains a part of Welsh social history. Thousands of men and women remember with affection the clinking of those glass bottles on the backs of the lorries and, above all, the expectation as they hurried home from school, of the delivery of yet another bottle of dandelion and burdock. It was an essential part of childhood.

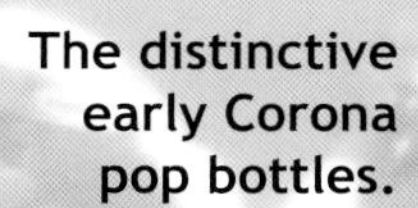

The distinctive early Corona pop bottles.

SOUTH WALES may be known for its steep-sided valleys which have often been a headache for planners and engineers. So too have the rivers that have flowed along them to the sea.

From Roman times many ingenious structures have eased the passage of travellers from east to west and back again, among them the original Neath River Bridge at Briton Ferry. Now dwarfed by the neighbouring M4 motorway crossing, Neath River Bridge replaced a centuries old ferry.

It was the biggest post Second World War civil engineering project in the whole of the UK.

Bridging the GAP

When it opened in October 1955 it shortened the journey time to Swansea avoiding a lengthy detour through Neath and Morriston and easing traffic congestion in both towns.

The images here show the bridge under construction and in the main image shortly after completion.

Towering

When it comes to bridges there is one South Wales structure that even to this day stands head and shoulders above the rest – literally!

It is the transporter bridge at Newport, a landmark that can be seen for at least 20 miles from both sides of the Bristol Channel. There are only seven others remaining in the world, including two in the UK, at Warrington and Middlesborough, but the one at Widnes, which crossed the River Mersey and Manchester Ship Canal, was demolished in 1961.

Eighteen transporter bridges were built in the world between 1893 and 1916 and the Newport bridge celebrated its centenary on September 12, 2006.

The Newport bridge still plays a vitally important role in the city's road network and after millions of pounds was spent on refurbishment looks set to do so well into the future. That is good news for the people of Newport for whom the bridge is an iconic landmark.

Today it is a Grade 1 listed structure and in 1998 a registered charity was set up, The Friends of Newport Transporter Bridge, which wants it given World Heritage status, like the similar bridge in Bilbao, Spain.

It is important historically because of its design, which is very unusual. Just at the turn of the 20th century transporter bridges were fashionable, particularly on the continent, where a French engineer, Ferdinand Arnodin, had built this type of bridge across the Seine at Rouen, at Rochefort and Nantes. He also built one at Bizerta, in Tunis, and is famed for his Pont Transbordeur at Marseilles, destroyed in the Second World War.

Members of Newport Corporation visited Rouen to inspect the bridge there and agreed to invite Arnodin to design a bridge for their town. Work began in the autumn of 1902 and four years later, without a life having been lost in constructing this Colossus of steel and wire, the bridge was officially opened by the Lord Lieutenant of the county, Viscount Tredegar, in 1906.

Despite the rain, thousands of Newport citizens arrived on the banks of the River Usk at noon for the great event. Almost imperceptibly at first the platform moved away from the bank and slowly gathered speed. The crowds cheered along the gaily decorated river banks, detonators were exploded and the band of the 4th Battalion of the South Wales Borderers played the national anthem.

The bridge is the lowest crossing on the Usk, connecting Pillgwenlly, a residential district, with the main industrial area and the docks. It is a link in the B4237 road and helps alleviate the congestion at Newport's only other road bridge across the river, a mile and a half upstream in the city centre.

Councillors chose the design because they wanted ships to be able to pass under the bridge, and the problem was the very low river banks at the best crossing point on the Usk. But it was not an easy decision and the debate over the proposed crossing went on for around 30 years.

Between 1869 and 1889 various schemes were put forward that would allow tall-masted ships to use the tidal river without hindrance. Parliamentary sanction was obtained by the Corporation in 1869 to operate a ferry, and again in 1889 to build and maintain a pedestrian subway, but neither scheme became a reality. The problem was again tackled in 1898, when proposals for ferries, subways, high-level, bascule, swing, lifting and rolling bridges were considered. It was then decided to build a transporter bridge, because it would cost considerably less than a subway capable of taking vehicles or a high-level bridge with sloping approaches.

transporter

The bridge was built to withstand a maximum wind speed of 110 mph and has been tested with a load of 120 tonnes. Its two towers are 242 ft high and 645 ft apart and the height of the stiffening girder, which actually spans the river, is 177 ft. The travelling platform is 33 ft long and 40 ft wide, forming a carriageway of 28 ft and two 6 ft footways.

On each bank there are four foundation piers. These are masonry wells mounted on steel shoes or curbs, and were sunk to depths varying from 78 ft to 86 ft by pneumatic pressure. When the shaft reached a depth of about 10 ft compressed air was used to keep out the water and it is believed that this was the first instance in Britain where masonry wells were sunk under air pressure. Two 35 bhp electric motors in the motor house at the eastern end of the bridge supply the power that moves the platform, which has a total weight of around 50 tonnes.

The truck that travels overhead has 60 steel wheels and is pulled to and fro by wires drawn by a winch worked by the electric motors. The driver controls the motion from the pilot house, which resembles a Chinese pagoda, built on the upstream side of the platform, but in an emergency the moving platform could be controlled from the motor house, where the instruments and controls are duplicated. At night, in accordance with the requirements of Trinity House, the towers and the travelling platform both carry navigation lights.

In 1900 Parliamentary sanction was obtained to go ahead with the building of the bridge at a cost of £65,603.

The first official trip over the bridge was a complete success, the crossing being made without the slightest vibration or swaying. That night one of the towers was illuminated and hundreds of people paid the halfpenny toll to cross the river.

Today the bridge is regarded as the most recognisable symbol in the City of Newport. It was the focal point for the millennium celebrations in 2000 and has been featured in films and television shows, including the 1959 film Tiger Bay, starring the 12-year-old starlet Hayley Mills.

But it has suffered from a number of problems in recent years.

The bridge was closed in 1985 because of wear and tear and did not reopen until 1995 after a £3 million refurbishment. Then it closed at the end of 2007 for another £1.2 million refurbishment and stayed shut until July 2010.

The bridge closed again in February 2011 because of operational problems and reopened the following June.

The bridge has a visitor centre run by the Friends who organise group and school visits to this landmark structure.

Its future appears to be in safe hands.

Span-tastic!

The George Street bridge that spans the River Usk at Newport.

The majestic sweep of the first M4 Severn Crossing.

The Cleddau Bridge, part of which collapsed during construction.

Bargoed railway viaduct, complete with train, 1991.

Time team

We hope you have enjoyed turning the pages of Slices of South Wales.

If you have then please let us know, but more importantly let your friends know of this fascinating publication. Better still, if you have any interesting tales or achievements you would like to see revived in a future edition, why not tell us about them and play your very own part in keeping our region's past alive. We're always keen to chat to our readers.

Slices of South Wales would not have been possible without the help of some very special people. Among them its compiler David Roberts, main writer Jonathan Isaacs, Phil Carradice, Herbert Williams, Roy Kneath, Keith Roberts, Grace Taylor, Stephen H Jones, Roger Gale, Jeff Childs, Cheryl Roberts, James Field, Brian Lee, Peter Massam, Philip Hale, Clydach Historical Society; Ashley Lovering, The South Wales Police Museum, Colin Scott, Neil Melbourne, Richard Brown, Anthony Isaac, David Beynon, Malcolm Ranson and Judy Totton.

We thank them all for their enthusiasm, encouragement and contribution.